Suffocated by Church

A gay man's journey to freedom.
A memoir by Paul Ward.

This work originated as **"Alice, An Autobiography"** This edition - Revised, edited and updated including a new cover design is cause for the revised title.

© Paul Ward, Caboolture, Australia. 2022

This is a work of fact, and as such names and places are those of actual people and locations.

Certain descriptions of abuse contained in this memoir are as I remember the experience. Others may challenge my memory. I respect their opinion.

It is not my intent to cause any harm or damage to people, mentioned or otherwise alluded to in the text. I simply present the facts as I have experienced them.

Any errors or concerns are to be addressed to myself: paulward.alice@gmail.com

Cover artwork by Amy Bonnici 2022.

Prologue to March 2022 Edition

Life, being so complex with different but inextricably linked and intertwined themes does, nevertheless, have distinct phases.

Themes for me include: Family and Church, Australian Culture, Working and Volunteer life, Spirituality, Sexuality, Relationships and Friendships, Locations, Thoughts and Feelings, Health, and Death.

Phases move along a continuum of time from early childhood and school years to young adulthood, early mature years, and middle age to older age.

These memoirs are set out following the life phases in pretty much chronological order. However, as alluded to above, these writings need to include focus or themed chapters. Phases and Themes are introduced along the way.

Scenes are used to add context and colour to the life story. Cultural insights emerge from the several themes including Church influence, family life and influences on my sexual and mental health.

As one wise and deeply spiritual woman once put it "all will be revealed."

Forward

In November 1981 I received a handwritten letter from a dear woman by the name of Martha McCredie. Martha wrote on the occasion of my imminent departure for several years in Papua New Guinea (PNG) as a missionary from the local catholic parish. In her letter Martha mentioned a 'wickery' apparently referring to a wall or house constructed of wicker work. When asked what she meant Martha replied, "All will be revealed." So it was, a few months later in April 1982 at Malala Mission on the North Coast Road of Madang PNG.

No doubt all will be revealed in these pages. You may have questions, as I did all those years ago in suburban Sydney.

My dear friend Louis Bonnici and his then fiancée, my sister, Anne Ward sent me a book of blank pages in which I began to write a journal. One of the first entries was a record of the night Martha's prophecy was revealed.

Dedication

This set of reflections and accounts of parts of my life is dedicated to Martha, Lou and Anne and the hundreds of people who have influenced my life, many of whom you will meet in the following pages.

My bibliography cannot be complete without particular mention of very significant others in my life. Naturally my dear parents Lloyd and Nola who through good times and rough supported me from my very beginning through childhood, growing to adulthood and into my later years, through my many stages of growth, many jobs, periods of doubt and struggles and through my relationships. Jennifer Herrick deserves special mention for all her support and loving care in recent decades of special friendship. My sisters Cathy and Anne and my brother Peter have always been around when needed. Finally, my dear Cheng Wee, my man and life support person, my life partner, 'hubby' and so much more. He is dear to my heart.

Since beginning this account and set of reflections on my life, both my dear parents, Nola and Lloyd have passed on to a new life beyond the struggles and material joys of this earthly existence. To them I remain ever grateful. Always in my heart.

Chapter 1
Growing up in Sydney in the mid-20th Century

Family, Church, Local area.

My parents met and married in the area south of Sydney around Botany Bay and Maroubra. Dad was a local butcher and mum lived nearby to the butcher shop; her mum suggested to the young Nola Campbell that she may be interested in young Lloyd. They had their Catholic faith in common and both belonged to the church social group, the CYO. The Catholic Youth Organisation was headquartered in the city and every Catholic parish in Sydney had a branch. The CYO organised social events, weekends away, dances and picnics. Members had to be practicing Catholics attending Church every Sunday. To gain admittance to the dance hall a that time, members had to get a ticket as they left church and hand it in at the door. The priest or CYO Chaplain attended weekly meetings which always opened with a set of prayers. He also attended the dances for a while. I'm told once he left the music turned to swing and the dance moves livened up somewhat. Boogie-woogie and Jive were popular. This was the post war period. Time to celebrate life and Christian faith!

Soon Lloyd Bailey Ward and Nola Margaret Campbell were Wed in Holy

Matrimony in the Church of the Holy Family at Maroubra. I was Baptised in that church too, an old man in black put salt on my tongue to make me cry then washed my head with cold water while I was dressed in a tight nappy and floral white boy's dress. My parents initially lived in a share house with a woman called 'Granny Clapham' and others. My first home was in that single room in a house on Gail Road. All the neighbours knew about me due to my crying mentioning to mum at the Masons community hall that thy heard Paul 'exercising his lungs'. Mum used to push me in a basket style pram to that hall shopping for cheap clothes or cloth to make clothing with. I remember women in hats peering into my pram gazing at me remarking how sweet I looked for a baby boy. Another early memory of mine is wriggling on the barber's chair. He had a wooden plank set up across the arms of the old barber chair so little children could sit on top. I was scared of falling off and didn't like the man in a white jacket attacking my head and hair with sharp scissors or a buzzing electric shears. They had to hold me down while I got my crew cut at the age of one or two. It must have been frightening. All those people looking, being held down, the noisy buzz, men chatting, the loose hairs irritating my neck and arms. I must have been sensitive to sound and touch back then.

    Soon we moved into a house of our own which belonged to mum's brother,

Uncle George. The brick home was in Pagewood a few kilometres from Maroubra and the Catholic church. Over many years Mum pushed my pram to Sunday Mass and back on an empty stomach as that was the rule back then in the 1950s. No food from midnight before Holy Communion on Sunday morning. Cold winter mornings in the dark and hot summer mornings, rain hail or shine. Mass was essential, even an Obligation for my parents and all good Catholics.

My first few years at Pagewood there were only the three of us. I played in the back yard on the grass, walked with mum to the shops or we caught a bus. She had to lift me up due to the very high steps. I had to hang on tightly especially with the double deckers as they didn't have a back door, the platform was just open for passengers to jump on or off. It was a little bit scary. Sometimes we would sit up on the back seat which faced sideways, and I could look out the back at the traffic. The 'fares please man' would come around selling tickets calling out 'fares please' as he struggled through the crowded bus. I remember walking up the street with mum to look through the fence to see the bus depot where all the buses were kept when they weren't busy. There was a very tall garage for the double deckers and the single deck buses were lined up neatly in rows out in the weather. Drivers had to check the fuel before leaving through the big wire gates. Pagewood Bus Depot was up on the next corner, so handy. One Saturday mum made a kite of brown paper and scraps of material for a tail and dad attached a long bit of string. He and I often went down to the field at the end of the street to fly our kite on windy days while mum cooked tea. Another day I was in the back yard when I saw the strangest thing crawling across the grass. It was spiky and looked like mum's brush, but I didn't think it could walk and wondered why it was out in the garden because mum always kept it on the dressing table in front of the mirror and her crystal glass jewellery holder. I walked inside to the kitchen and told mum I saw her brush walking in the grass. I think she was surprised. She came out to see and told me it was an Echidna and not to touch it. When Dad came home, he put it in a cardboard box and put grass in with it. He walked up to the corner phone box and called Tooronga Zoo. Later a man from the zoo came and took spike the echidna away. Sometimes the girl next door who was much older than me, about age 5 or 6, would trick me and grab my arm and twist it. I would cry a bit each time. I soon learnt to run away from her even if she called me a sissy or weak boy. I wanted to be brave and strong but the arm wringing game was too rough for me. I think her name was Theresa Green, someone else lived down the street, the Brown family. One day a little girl from our street disappeared and the police came searching. She was found dead in an old fridge where she had been hiding and the door closed on her. Her brother was sad, me too. It was the law after that that old fridges had to have the door taken off if left in the street for collection by the council. I was told never to get in a fridge or in a dangerous place. If I felt scared, I shouldn't do it. Haircuts were different.

    We soon moved to a brand-new house in Matraville. I remember it being built and looking over the construction site as for a four-year-old boy it was so exciting! We moved in there in 1959 just before I began school and before Cathy was born. Peter came along a year and a month later so Mum had me just beginning school and two little ones. It must have been difficult for her. I soon learnt to walk to and from school myself. It was about a 30 min walk, from home down the street, past the European Migrant Hostel, up and over a hill and down the other side, past the old quarry which we called the dump, around the corner by the Post Office, down the main road to the school grounds. The school had a low brick fence and three classrooms in one small block. There was Kindergarten, first class and second class when I started in 1960. A new classroom block and school hall were built and the school expanded with the growing population. The people from the hostel moved into the general community and the suburb of Matraville developed. A new church was designed and constructed. St Agnes' Matraville opened in 1966, one of the first in Australia blessed and opened after the Second Vatican Council (Vatican II). My sister Anne was born early in 1964 completing the family of six when I was aged 10.

By that time, I was an Altar Boy serving the priest at Mass, ringing bells and knocking over tall brass flower vases. It felt important to be standing by the priest. By the age of 15, I was the senior server and training new boys in the skill of lighting the thurible and holding the cruets for the priest. At least I didn't have to teach them Latin as that had been done away with by 1965.

I had to serve at the 6:45 morning Mass on Wednesday mornings every Wednesday. I was often the only boy there out of our group of four or five boys. Dad walked me the kilometre or so up to Malabar church a few times then I was on my own. He'd wake me at 6:20 or so and I'd trot up, often through the morning fog past the long-wet grass which surrounded the sewage incinerator. I was the only person on the roads at that hour. It was sort of peaceful.

Danger among locals

One morning a man in his 40's walked behind me. He followed me on several Wednesdays then one day he walked close to me and started to talk to me. He said he was going to the church too and he had seen me there on

Wednesdays and Sundays. He asked if it's ok for him to walk with me and he would keep me safe in the dark as I was walking alone. He had been seen at the school fence handing out boiled sweets to children, but Sister asked him to keep away for some reason. I never took sweets from him at the fence. His name was Mr Mann. On our walks he impressed me with his worldly knowledge of church matters. Beyond my youthful understanding. He introduced me to the concept of the Universal Church saying that due to different time zones around the world it was morning or night in different places and that somewhere around the world people were attending Mass at any minute or hour. He said it was a glorious thing that Catholics were all over the world in Europe, Asia, Africa, the Pacific and in North and South America. He helped me with Latin too. Sometimes he would invite me to his house, but I was always busy or expected home. However, one Saturday afternoon in summer when I was about twelve or so he convinced me to visit. His house was near my family home. It was only half built with a blank wall at the front. Some people couldn't afford to finish off their house due to being poor and unemployed. He had one big room with a wooden table and chairs and a kitchen in the corner and no walls in the big room. He gave me milk and biscuits to eat and drink while he went away to have a shower. I saw him walking around in his underwear and peeping around the corner looking at me from several feet or a few yards away. He came back fully dressed and asked if I wanted to stay some more. I said no I had to go home to help mum with cooking tea. So, I left and walked home. He never touched me. When I got home from my walk mum asked why I took so long. I said I had visited Mr Mann. She asked who he was, and I told her he used to walk with me to church and he was a friendly man. She told me not to visit him or strangers ever again. I was to walk another way and go down other streets rather than my usual route. I may have noticed him in church sometimes, but we never met or spoke again.

    Another time at a similar age I used to take my siblings to play in the park. Sometimes I'd go alone. One afternoon several older boys who were about 14 or 15 or so approached me in the park as I walked home past a big old tree. Some gathered around me. I felt ok and some were quite handsome I thought. However, they asked me personal questions of a sexual nature. They asked me to join them in their friendship group. They met on weekends in a single man's home which was along the main road near the church. They said they were nude and played games with each other and the older man. They said it was so much fun and I would make a good playmate. I began to feel unsafe with them but not physically threatened by them. I said I couldn't go to the man's place as it was so far to walk. They said to tell my parents I was going on a walk to visit a friend's house and would stay for lunch or a snack. I didn't want to go. I left and walked quickly home and once again mum asked where I had been. I said I had been to the park and some boys asked me personal questions and invited me to a strange man's house. Saying it was a boy's friendship circle. Mum once again told me not to go. I said I was not interested any way because it sounded a bit strange to me. She agreed. I never saw them again and always looked around when I was walking near the park or that old tree.

Perpetual Light and the Fires of Hell

St Agnes' school stands on the main road through Matraville. Buses from the city to this location were the route 337 Botany Cemetery service. The Cemetery was the end of the line in more ways than one. It was on the cliffs above the shores of Botany Bay near the beach where the American scientist Mr James Matra and the English Botanist Joseph Banks stepped ashore after rowing across the flat waters of the bay in 1770. The two were crew of Lieutenant Cook's ship Endeavour which had landed on the southern shores of Botany Bay. Legend has it that the Englishman didn't want to get his shoes wet so his dear friend had the job of jumping out of the ships' boat and pulling it ashore thus being the first known foreigner to step upon the sandy northern shores of that Bay. For this effort he was honoured by James Cook naming the locality Matraville. The settlers of the First Fleet in Sydney Cove (part of Sydney Harbour) set out south on foot down to Matraville in 1788 only to discover crew of French explorers set up camp on a headland just to the east of Matraville. They had buried a Christian chaplain there. So, to this day a plot of land remains French Territory and the location named after the French Captain La Perouse. On the opposite headland is the Botany Cemetery and Crematorium.

    Sitting in the primary school classroom gazing out the window to the south we could see a tall thin tower or stack over in the distance near the cemetery. The flame never went out. It glowed day and night every day. Being a Catholic school, we prayed a lot. One of the prayers was for the dead. I knew they were buried in that cemetery on the next hill. The prayer asked God for the perpetual light to shine upon them. One day someone asked Sr Julian our religion teacher and school headmistress about the perpetual light. What was it? She said perpetual means it goes on forever and never goes out. I saw the flame and was sure God put that light next to the cemetery to shine on the dead people. I never asked why dead people needed a light seeing as they were buried in the sand. I trusted Sister and never questioned her or God. Later when I was a teenager, I saw that Boral refinery was next to the cemetery and the eternal flame was actually a safety device burning off gas in the production of bitumen and petroleum products. God didn't put it there for the dead. My faith began to be questioned in a small way. If that flame wasn't the perpetual light of God, what was? There was no answer. No Sister to ask. The sisters wore black uniforms including a veil and covered neck and forehead. We guessed Nuns had ears otherwise their glasses might fall off. They seemed to float along too, although I did see they wore black shoes so I knew they must have had feet and legs. Another mystery we learnt was a bit good but also scary. About angels: We each had a guardian angel sitting on our right shoulder who told us all the good things to do or say. However, there was a devil or bad angel sitting on our left shoulder trying to tell us to do wrong things. Some of us tried to bash the left shoulder angel but it wouldn't work Sister said. We just had to pray to God and listen to our guardian angel. God could see everything too, just like Santa who kept a list if we were naughty or nice. I was pretty good because Santa gave me things under the Christmas tree each year. Though some children got better stuff like pump up scooter. One year when I was older the last thing Santa gave me was a boy's bike, but by then I knew dad worked on it all summer restoring an old one just for me. I knew Sister liked me because I got to do extra work after school just for her. I was allowed into her office to collect all the rubbish papers and take them to the burner at the back of the classrooms. Some people called it an incinerator, but it was a rubbish burner. It was hot once I started the fire sometimes, I'd burn my fingertips. Walking home I had soot in my nostrils and a dirty face and mum had to wash my uniform and try to dry it before the next day.

    Also, being a good Catholic boy, I had to make my first Confession before my First Holy Communion. As the old church was miles away from the school there was a temporary church in the school hall while a permanent church building was constructed. Therefore, my first confession was held in the school building outside sisters' office in the broom closet. Yes. We all had to line up along the corridor and take our turns to go in and kneel next to the Priest, Fr James Munday who was sitting there in the dark. I thought it was strange to see him there, sort of like hiding in the broom closet listening to our secret sins. I couldn't think of anything I had done which needed the forgiveness of God and the Priest in the Sacrament of Confession. I tried hard to make up something he would believe an innocent seven-year-old boy would have done. I began: Bless me Father for I have sinned; this is my first confession. "Yes, my son" he replied. "I took a small blue marble while no one was looking, out in the playground." He said, "For that say one Hail Mary and ask for forgiveness. I did and said I would never sin again. I hope Jesus understood I had to make up something otherwise I would have to see the Priest in the dark closet again. My confession itself was a lie. Next came the First Holy Communion. Sister gave us practice in the church hall. We lined up and knelt at the altar rails and closed our eyes as she came along pretending to be the priest and pretending to give us a small white wafer on our tongue. I didn't peep but I guess Sister pressed her finger on our tongues. Yuck. But she was a Nun and we were in the church and there would have been no germs, so it was ok. Nevertheless, Mum made sure I cleaned my teeth well before tea that night as soon as I got home. Sister put her finger on 30 mouths in alphabetical order and I was near the end near the boy Zammit. The next Sunday was first Holy Communion Day and I had to wear a clean white shirt and my school shorts and freshly cleaned black shoes. I had to hold my hands together with the right thumb over the left. The priest said, "Corpus Christie" and we said "amen". I swallowed the wafer, but one boy took it out of his mouth just to see what Jesus looked like. He looked like a shiny white wafer circle about 15mm in diameter with a PX stamped on it. Pax Christie. Pax for person or body and the X because they couldn't fit "Christie" on such a small space. After communion the leftovers of Jesus were put in a golden container and locked in a box on the wall behind the altar next to a red light. It wasn't the perpetual light but a different one to show that Jesus was locked away there. Poor man I thought. He came to earth to visit us and we lock him in a box on the wall. I never did understand how he could be in a piece of white wafer for me and in others for other people and there were hundreds and thousands of little wafers of Jesus all over the world, but just one Jesus. So strange and difficult to understand. Sister said it was a Sacred Mystery. She would say that to questions she couldn't answer. "It's a mystery, children". The whole church was a mystery. Same as Santa. How could he be all over the world in one night and no one saw him? Soon the new sandstone church was built over the dusty base of the quarry next to the schoolhouse. That sure put an end to the horrifying sight of the smoke from the fires of hell next to the school. Every Friday we walked all around the school in a procession saying the rosary and prayers about "save us from the fires of Hell". We happened to get up to that part as we walked over the dusty old quarry and it looked like smoke rising up all over our clothes and our skin. Yet another washing job for mum.

Mum made all our school uniforms, tunics for Cathy and shirts for me, from material and using patterns bought at Maroubra uniform shop. We had a sewing machine at the kitchen window. The shorts were too difficult to make at home, so mum and dad bought them off the hanger for me. The brand name was Stamina. I asked what stamina meant and was told it was the ability to keep going, something I found difficulty with. We had to clean our shoes with a cleaner named Gumption, another word I had trouble with as it meant strength and staying power. However, I did pride myself in the whitest sandshoes in the class if not the whole school.

The boys had to go to the Marist Brothers' schools at Daceyville and Pagewood from grade three till the end of school days while the girls stayed with the sisters till grade six then to the sisters at Maroubra Junction. The state education system changed during my early years and the Wyndham Scheme was introduced which meant we had a choice to continue to year 12 rather than leave at year 10 at age 15. The scheme also had the concept of streaming of more intelligent students together above less intelligent ones. We had Black, Green and Gold, the school colours. I was in the Green stream, in the middle. The boys in Black were looked upon as superior and more likely to go on to years 11 and 12 then University. The greens may have had a chance to finish year 10 with good results while the boys in the Gold classes were just filling up desks to make it to age 15 to drop out of education and may have luck getting a job working on the roads or garbage trucks. I tried my very best not to be a garbage truck man. My friend Phillip joined the council workers on a garbage truck. He worked for two weeks and got a bad back never to work again. Not that I was to know that at the time. I wanted to be a teacher when I grew up.

    Some of my heroes were the brothers who dedicated their lives to education. In primary school Brother Cleophas was the headmaster and grade six teacher. He looked friendly and wise with a glowing round face and thick hair. One Saturday I took myself to visit him at school just to say hello. He asked me how I was getting home, but I didn't know. He helped me find the way to the bus stop and made sure I was on the right bus home. He told me if ever I was going somewhere, I had to have a plan to get there and a plan to get home or away too. I'll never forget that. Cleophas wasn't his real name it was his name as a Marist Brother. Back then they took the name of their hero saint. Another Brother had the name of Roland. He told us in year 10 that he liked seeing us get changed on the athletic field and at the pool because he noticed our mature chests and saw we were not young boys anymore. Another Brother was my high school Commerce teacher Br Richard. The boys called him 'big dick' for some reason. He would introduce the topic and ask us to take notes then he'd fall asleep at the desk till the bell rang. Sometimes he's hit us on the bum with the yard ruler. Some years later when I was a young adult with the Matraville CYO group we went exploring and looking around the night spots of Sydney, as older teenagers do. We didn't dare go into a pub or anything, just walked the main street of Kings Cross. Brother Richard was seen by some of the Pagewood old boys standing on the footpath near a wall as if he was looking for someone.

Chapter 2
First period of Vocational Calling.

Brother Paul

Back in 1970 the Sydney priest Vocation director, Fr Kerry Bayada, visited the school and some boy put my name down to see him but I wasn't interested in being a priest. However, he suggested I should ask about being a Brother. So, I asked. The next year I was off, leaving home at the age of 15, going to a little country town, Mittagong, in the Southern Highlands to the south of Sydney. I packed my suitcase and dad saw me off at Central Station on the train.

I arrived in the late dusk at Mittagong after a quiet and long train trip from Sydney. All I knew was that a man named Brother Valerius was to meet me along with several other boys. The train departed and the other passengers disbursed leaving a few lads who gradually gravitated toward the station building in the dark and wondered where Brother was. We were all about age 15, strangers to each other. It was an eerie feeling standing there alone with strangers who were to be part of my life for the next few years. Brother arrived with a torch light. He had been searching the opposite platform and the carpark and eventually joined us huddled there in the dark corner. Someone asked him who he was searching for. He said he was expecting 22 of us but there were only 7 who turned up. We were told to jump up onto the back of the red tip truck which we did. I managed to sit on a lump of clay which made an indelible stain on my new calico work trousers. I leant on my case as Brother drove us the few miles from town to the Marist Brothers Juniorate site. The Juniorate was the school community of several brothers and the students (juniors) of years 11 and 12 who were to eventually train to be young Marist Brothers. Also, at the small farm was a Marist Priest, a French man, Dom Paul David, who lived alone and the cook Mrs Jones and her family who lived in a small cottage. We weren't to speak to them at all apart from saying good morning or evening if they spoke to us. Mrs Jones was a good cook and a friendly woman. Her kitchen consisted of wood fired stoves and a big walk-in fridge. There was a pantry between the kitchen and the dining room and a door from the dining room into the chapel. The professed men sat at the rear, year 12 boys on the left and year 11 on the right side. Anyone who was late had to kneel in the aisle, a favourite occupation of mine. Once I decided to sit in a different pew but Brother told me not to sit there and to kneel on the hard timber floor. I had apparently sat on the wrong side. That's when I learnt about hierarchy in the church even if we were all brothers.

Our dormitory would have easily accommodated over one hundred boys on beds a metre apart in four or five rows. We totalled 21. Each of us was allocated one single bed and a locker. There was no privacy at all. A set of stairs in the centre joined the dorm to the lower floor on which were the four classrooms. Below that, on the ground floor was the large recreation hall with an old radiogram which was permanently tuned to the catholic pop music station 2SM, in one corner. Some of the hits included: My Sweet Lord, Mr Bojangles, I hear you knocking, and that one by Arlo Guthrie - something about a restaurant? In the other corner was a worn-out snooker table. Hung from the roof was a twin rope a sort of flying trapeze on which some of the stronger lads swung from time to time. Outside the hall along the full length of the brick building was a parapet or edgeless veranda. At one end of the hall was the kitchen, pantry, dining room and chapel. At the opposite end was the grassed oval beyond which we weren't to venture unless invited and accompanied by a Brother. That forbidden zone housed the Novitiate and dairy. We were also forbidden to walk beyond the gates except one Saturday a month when we could walk into town for a milkshake or post a letter. One of the old retired brothers had a hobby garden. Br Valerius was the headmaster and community superior. Br Bede taught maths. Brother Anthony taught Economics and another taught Science. Once, with Br Benedict, we went on an excursion to the limestone

Wombeyan Caves part of the Great Dividing Range, south of the Blue Mountains.

We were able to have family visitors once a term and my mum and dad visited with Cathy and Peter and little Anne who was about five then. Cathy made me some coconut ice and brought it all the way in a blue plastic container which I still have, though the sweets are long gone. Each Junior had tasks and jobs were changed monthly. I was a bell ringer, wood chopper, boiler keeper, pantry boy, and dining room attendant. I loved setting the tables and making the butter flat in silver butter tureens. I had the job of putting the bread out of the freezer of a night-time after supper and night prayer. One night I forgot till the next morning when I ran down to the freezer and quickly put the bread loaves directly into the oven and I made sure the fire was burning hot and strong. At breakfast that winter's day I served bread with burnt paper clinging to a very crisp crust and frozen centre. I was given other duties after that. How could I have forgotten? So embarrassing!

One afternoon a year 12 Junior named Ken was chatting and mouthing off about some opinion and I wanted to have my say. He wouldn't stop so I thought one way to stop his mouth was to hit it. I punched him in the face. He then raved on saying it was the first time in the history of the Juniorate that any boy had hit another let alone a year 11 hit a year 12 lad. Blah

Blah Blah.. Brother told me not to bother Ken again. I do recall digging out the sludge trap after that. At least the stain on my trousers blended in with the kitchen sewage mud and my boots got dirty, a sign of masculinity. Another time I felt alone and lonely. Some of the boys had gone out with permission. Others were around but I felt I couldn't talk to them or join them. Two very handsome lads with long blond hair and muscular bodies were favourites of Brother Val. This night they were sitting in an abandoned car talking. I grabbed a 9Lb (4kg) sledgehammer from the wood pile and took it to the car and belted the rear bumper bar as hard as I could. The young guys inside jumped out so fast I was shocked. They asked what I was up to and why I hit the car. I said I was lonely, and I guess I was jealous that I had no-one to talk to or hang out with. I reflect now that I didn't really have any friends there. I spoke to others while performing duties such as sweeping the floor or loading up huge logs into the boiler. One night in the boiler room I mentioned to the other lad that on the recent weekend when we were allowed out, I visited Campbelltown, a southern Sydney suburb. He asked why I went there and what happened. I made up a 'cock and bull' story. I had nothing to do but sit on a park bench waiting for the return train. While there this young pretty woman approached and asked if I was feeling lonely. I said yes. She said I could go visit her for an hour to fill in time and for ten dollars I could experience my first sexual act with a girl. I was so shy but was eager to see what it was like, so I paid her the cash which I had saved for lunch. The other fellow didn't seem to believe me. He was 16 going on 17 and actually I found him very attractive, he being older and more muscular than myself. I wanted to impress him I guess, or to deny my attraction to him. He asked me the name of the girl. I said her name was Alice McDonald. I had already confected this story while sitting on that hard bench in a park on McDonald Street Campbelltown. The mind of a lonely 15-year-old boy can make up almost anything, especially when he is innocent and naive. The story was heard up in the library that night! The head Brother was informed and I was called to his office to explain. He said I had no need to make up stories and that I should go to the Priest to confess leading others into scandal. A young man, really a young teenager could survive the daily life of work and study and prayer without close mates. I followed the routines and tried my best. I was often late for chapel or slow at other things. The economics teacher spoke quickly, and we nicknamed him Speed. I was slow working in class one day and he came to me and whispered in my ear: "speed for speed". I had to focus on the textbook and answering questions. Another lesson was Maths. I was the only boy in Level 3 Mathematics and was taught by Br Bede. I didn't get the basic concepts so one day he said Paul, I have only one question today. If you get it correct you can go early, if not you will not have any more maths lessons. - The question was: "what is a number?" After 40 minutes of guessing I still didn't get it. No more Maths! Such a relief. At least I wouldn't be a maths teacher. Probably not an economics teacher either. I would have been happy to just teach religion and tell others who Jesus was and the Love of God. Maybe I would be a missionary in some exotic location for the remainder of my life trekking through the jungle visiting remote tribes with the Word of God.

Mother's Day came around soon enough and I didn't have a card for her as the newsagent had closed and I hadn't bought a card in advance, so I walked into town on the permitted Saturday and found the tourist bureau open. I purchased a postcard showing a picture of Mittagong town and mailed it to mum. I felt lonely and homesick at the time. Then the Provincial Leader visited from Sydney and interviewed each of us. He asked me why I wanted to be a Marist brother. I said after some reflection that I wanted to be a teacher. He said anyone could be a teacher I didn't have to be a brother. I thought again and said, "to tell others about Jesus and the catholic faith." He said no that's not it either. I asked him what the correct answer was. He said it was for myself so that I would get to heaven. I thought that was selfish but didn't say so because he was the Provincial superior. Shortly after that I spoke with Brother Valerius and said I was thinking I should go home to my family. He picked up the phone and spoke to the local operator who put a connection through to my home and dad answered. I said I spoke with Brother and had decided to go home. Dad sounded a bit sad but a bit relieved too, saying "bag and baggage son?" I guessed he meant 'for good" or permanently rather than a visit. I said yes. Brother told dad he would call again with the details of the train once a seat had been booked for me. Before I left, I asked brother if I should stay after all because who would do my job chopping wood for the fire. He said not to worry he and the others would take care of the tasks. It was my job now to pack and go home and move on with my life. I'll never forget that lesson in life, to move on and don't worry about the others especially management, they can do without me. I was home at Matraville the following weekend. I don't remember others seeing me off at the station or any farewell speeches. Surely some of the others wished me well. I was to find paid employment for the first time in my life but for the time being I was home in the care of my family.

    The Postmaster General's Department (PMG) was my first employer. From the middle of 1971 I was an office boy, a clerical assistant grade one. I was sorting internal mail for the Finance and Accounting section of the PMG in the Sydney office above the old Imperial shopping Arcade in Pitt Street. I worked on the mail desk with a woman called Beryl and we opened bags of mail each morning and distributed the contents around the two floors of the office. Sometimes Mr Kevin Ryan the manager asked me to run errands across the city with a leather briefcase. I felt important doing that. The office hours were strictly 8:25 to 4:31pm, seven hours and 21 minutes a day. If, or when, I arrived late even by a minute or two I had to sign under the red line in the attendance book and each fortnight had to explain in detail why I was late. I was usually docked 5 or 6 minutes pay because of the 'late bus'. Most people were union members and didn't want to be seen working past the 4:31 mark so they tidied their desks, brushed hair, put on jackets and so on right up to 4:30 then stood at the main door till the clock hit the 31´ mark then they literally ran to the lifts and waited up to five minutes as every one of the about 230 clerks and assistants finished all at the same time. We didn't get paid for an extra 2 or 3 minutes and couldn't make up time from being late to working extra till say 4:35. No way! We would have been reported to Dulcie the union Rep and got into trouble with her, not that I was in the union.

Alice, one of the young women had a boyfriend who was in a rock band and he needed a new drum kit which was on special, so Alice asked me one pay day if I could lend her $200 and she'd pay me back later. I said sure at 10% interest. The next Monday she gave me back $210 in cash, and I asked if her boyfriend got the drums, he hadn't. I felt sad for Alice and wanted to waive the interest, but she said a deal is a deal, so I kept the cash. Our pay in those days was $37.50 a week paid fortnightly in cash. I enjoyed that work, it was easy and ran to a routine everyday Monday to Friday. At the office people told me if I got the HSC, I could be a clerk and get more pay due to higher duties, so I went to night school at Maroubra four nights a week. I didn't do study and went to the CYO at Matraville on Wednesday nights and Saturday afternoons. I failed every subject in 1972.

    I would pay my parents an amount in board for food and so on and I'd do tasks at home such as helping with washing and sweeping floors. I was about 16 to 17, grew a thick black beard and was popular in the office. I went to church every Sunday with my family. I remember Mrs Smith pumping out 'We stand for God' on the organ as we climbed the stairs to church. Dad was in the Society of St Vincent De Paul and they had meetings on Tuesday nights after tea. He would organise the collection plates and sell the Catholic Weekly and pious objects on the church steps after Mass. Sometimes I'd help set up the table or take a plate around. Most people put 20 cents or even 50 cents on the cash plate and up to five dollars or so in the envelopes. I helped count the envelopes in the priests' back room sometimes. My favourite part was sorting them into numerical order. I was also fascinated by the coin separator device. Sometimes Sister would get dad to mow the grass in front of the convent and the sisters would give us a glass of water.

In a corner near an old set of timber and brass stairs near the Pitt Street entrance of the Sydney GPO was stored two sets of reference books, one being the Australian Electoral Roll set out by Divisions or Federal Electorates, the other was the complete set of Australian white pages and pink pages Telephone Directories. I loved reading these and following patterns of names or localities or prefix numbers or area codes. The books and their contents were interesting, indeed fascinating. Another resource was the single volume Australian Postcode book which listed localities and place names in order of State and Territory then in strict alphabetical order from Abbotsford to Zetland. The old brass and timber stairs were also quite fascinating as they formed part of the original 1890s GPO building number 1 Martin Place.

Although I had only 45 minutes for lunch break, it was only a few hundred metres down Pitt Street from the Imperial

Centre in which I worked for the PMG. The GPO formed the NSW State HQ of the PMG. My connection to the building was almost spiritual so much so that I often dream of those stairs and the dark corridors and lead-sealed front steps off Martin Place. Such was the fascination that I dream of the lifts too, more on that later.

Brother Paul (II).

During the Christmas season of 1972 and into the new year of 1973 I once again felt a calling or vocation to be a brother in the Church. I found those phone books and searched the listing: Sydney > Catholic Church > Religious Communities > Male. I ran my index finger down the list past familiar names or groups such as Marist, Franciscan, St John of God, and Divine Word Missionaries and so on. I noticed the Order of the Society of Saint Gerard Majella who had only one house in Sydney, located at 106 Kerrs Road Kemps Creek, phone number 606 1007. James Bond was number 007 but that was little to do with a calling to religious life for me, though I was a 007 fan. I could also do number or numeral games in my head with the 106, 606, 007 and all that. Kemps Creek sounded exotic to me, hadn't heard of it as a Sydney suburb. I wasn't familiar with western Sydney at all. Also, my middle name was Gerard, of Gerard Majella fame, the Saint protector of

Mothers, especially new mothers and children. My parents had given me that name to protect me as a child and in thanks to Gerard for prayers answered to God for mum's protection in her pregnancy with me in 1954. It all seemed fascinating and as if it were meant to be. I was called to be a Brother of the Society of Saint Gerard. I found 10 cents and called the number. I asked to speak with the Vocations Director as I knew the Marists had one and the Archdiocese of Sydney had one, therefore every religious organisation in the Church would have one. I was surprised when the man who answered the phone said the Brothers didn't have a Vocations Director and I heard him ask around for the best person to speak with. I was then transferred to a Brother Stephen Robinson with whom I spoke saying I felt a calling to be a Brother and could I speak with him. He said he would arrange a meeting with someone called Brother John Sweeney. An appointment was made, and I took a train all the way out to St Mary's near Penrith for dinner. Brother John told me one of his men would meet me at the station at four o'clock on Saturday afternoon and drive me out to the Monastery. The driver didn't introduce himself or if he did, I didn't get his name. He was dressed in what I'd call gardener's clothes, a check shirt, calico style long trousers, and heavy boots. He had a kind and gentle face and spoke clearly but politely blocked my curious questions saying I was best to ask Brother John so the car ride to the chicken and tomato farm rural fringe of Sydney was a quiet one. Perhaps I guessed he was a gardener in part due to what Brother John said, "one of my men". The driver didn't look like a brother due to his casual nature and outfit.

    We approached the monastery from a long road. It stood sprawled across a low hilltop at the end of a pine tree lined entrance road. The hill was covered in freshly cut neat lawn. Several cars were parked on a gravel driveway outside. This tangerine Holden Torana made up four next to two other standard sedans and a rather grander looking semi luxury vehicle nearest the front entrance. I was shown into the brothers' lounge room which has cream and white colour themes a yellow-coloured lounge and chairs, coffee tables and some religious art hung on the walls.

    While I was waiting for Brother John, I was offered tea or coffee but had a cold water. A young brother arrived dressed like a priest in full soutane with a wide ribbon around his waist and shiny black shoes. He introduced himself as Brother John Love and said that Brother John Sweeney asked him to show me around the place. I followed in curious excitement. The building had two wings to each side of the main brick cottage which was obviously the original homestead. A third wing formed a T shape off the rear of the main cottage section. That wing housed the dining room and library and a small dormitory of a few teenage boys aged about 15 or 16. Tall thin lads who were apparently still in school. The wing to the left housed several rooms on either side of a corridor. These were the Professed Brothers rooms. Down to the right young brothers lived, they were Scholastics or students of university. They had their own bathroom which was opposite the Chaplain's rooms. At the far end of the right wing was the chapel. Outside was a laundry block and sort of a storeroom or shed. The whole property would have sat on a few acres or a hectare or two.

    We were soon back to the formal or front lounge room and a pair of sliding doors were closed to shut out the cottage from the remainder of the community buildings. The young brother John introduced the senior Brother John and escorted us into a private dining room at the end of the short hallway past a very impressive office and a private bathroom and kitchen which had been converted or renovated to have large stoves and fridges. The private dining room had a dark timber wardrobe along one wall and a bed in a dark corner. We sat at a small round table on tall wooden chairs. The table was set with fine china and stainless-steel cutlery on starched white linen. Brother John said grace and we enjoyed pumpkin soup with a bread roll, roast chicken and vegetables with a rich gravy followed by ice-cream on banana. The young Br John served us with a linen cloth draped over his left arm. I was careful not to spill gravy or crumbs on the plush carpeted floor.

I used the bathroom after dinner and joined Brother John in his office. He sat with his back to the windows which overlooked the garden and I sat opposite his huge timber desk in a stiff but comfortable chair. I could feel sweat on my palms and tried to pat them dry with my handkerchief which mum had ironed especially. I had a pair of rosary beads in my left pocket and my train ticket in my shirt pocket and a few dollars cash and my weekly ticket for use from the city back home. My utmost focus was on this tall and powerful looking man. One with knowledge and authority. He asked me if I had any questions and I said I did. If they didn't have a vocation director, who was he, the Provincial leader? He said they didn't have provinces due to the size of the Order; he called an Institute. They did have regional houses including one being established in Bunbury near Perth WA and one in Bowral in the NSW Southern Highlands. They had regional or community superiors. I asked if he wasn't a Vocations Director or a Provincial who was he. I almost fell off the chair and a sudden stream of sweat ran down my back when he told me. He was The Very Reverend Brother John Sweeney SSG, Founder Superior General. A founder Superior General!! Wow I had just had dinner with a future Saint. All founders of Religious Orders were Saints such as St Francis or so on. I then asked if he usually lived in Rome because all world-wide Superior Generals lived in the Vatican. He said he lived in the cottage there and our dining room was in fact his bedroom converted for the occasion of my visit. All this grandeur was most impressive to this wet behind the ears young teenage catholic. I was in utter awe.

    On his intercom he summoned the Brother Consultors to his office. He told them that he considered me to be a good potential brother but asked what they thought. Brothers Andrew Robinson, his twin Stephen Robinson, Brother Lawrence Cross, Brother Joseph Pritchard, and Brother Maurice Taylor crowded around the door to the office with Lawrence objecting with respect that they needed to be notified of such a recommendation in advance of a regular extraordinary meeting of the Consultors. John Sweeney insisted that it was his personal recommendation as the Superior General that I be accepted into the formation program, that I would begin as a Postulant not as a Novice and as such didn't need formal approval, as approval of the consultors was required only for an aspirant to enter the Novitiate. I felt that some were not happy but agreed.

    Brother John then suggested to the others that the tall pine trees at the entrance to the property needed a good soaking of water as it was dry. Some of the others said that they had lessons to prepare and papers to work on and asked if it couldn't be done on the next weekend. John Sweeney insisted and as I was driven out to the station by Brother Mark, I saw some men in the dark watering the trees.

The next weekend I was settling into the back room with the teenagers who were enrolled in the Marist Brothers School at Mittagong. Brother John Sweeney told me I couldn't attend there as I had been at Mittagong just a few years before. So, I was to attend the Parramatta Marist School at Westmead. All this because the SSG run all boys school at Greystanes near Pendle Hill was yet only up to year 10. I was to be in year 12 having done half of year 11 in 1971. I was assured I could cope as I had also worked 18 months with the PMG and so had worldly knowledge beyond that of the other teenagers. Brother Lawrence was the Principal of the SSG School, and he took me personally to the Principal of Parramatta Marist to formalise my enrolment which was accepted even though the school term had already begun. There were limited places and I had to do Science and other subjects such as Modern History which I felt were not for me.

I couldn't see the point of learning history as it had already passed. I just didn't understand the importance of historical knowledge. Why remember names and localities and dates off by rote? I did miss the introductory week but still! The Brother teaching history would enter the year 12 room of 30 young men in their late teens and begin with ten minutes of questioning and punishment. He would start at the front left near the windows and work his way down one row and along another till he got to the end of row four. I sat in the back corner, near the end hoping to get a repeat question so I could guess a correct answer. If a boy failed to answer immediately, he would have to stand, if a boy hesitated, he stood, if an answer was wrong, he stood. In the first weeks a few boys stood, he then became increasingly quicker and intolerant of errors. Those of us who had to stand were humiliated enough in front of our peers. Brother then proceeded to put us down. A few weeks later he had progressed (or regressed) to hitting our hands with a flat ruler, then our fingers with the edge of the ruler, then a quick sharp whack on our buttocks with the flat side of a metre rule, then worst seemed to be the sharp edge of a ruler down our backside so that it was somewhat painful to sit comfortably through the remaining 50 minutes of his drivel. I had had enough one morning and gathered my books ready to leave the room if he wanted to hit me again. He ordered me to bend over and be hit. I refused. He said he would send me to the principal if I refused his order. I said,

"Brother I am going to the principal" and took my books and left the room. I walked straight down to the principal's office and asked to see Brother Lawrence. I was asked why but said it's a confidential matter. So, I waited through the next period and got to see him soon enough. I outlined the events and feelings in the history class saying there were 18-year old's who could be called up through conscription to fight for Australia in Vietnam, others had full beards. We all were old enough to be fathers. I said Brother "if we don't know our history, that's our problem and we shouldn't be punished like that by the teacher." He said he would speak with the brother at lunch time. I then went out to have lunch with my year 12 mates on the hill overlooking the student's car park which was larger than the staff car park. We were permitted to smoke there on the hill during lunch break as long as we were out of sight of the younger students. The next day the history teacher entered the room and proclaimed, "Boys we will not have questions from now on because if you don't know your history it's your problem." My classmates smiled and turned towards my corner giving the thumbs up. I was a hero for just one day. I felt good and appreciated.

    I was told that the Brothers of St Gerard would support me in any way to help with my HSC education. I felt confident. I felt welcome and important. The Society paid my full fees and book allowance and stationery requirements. The Brothers supplied me with a full summer school uniform of trousers and two grey shirts, and school tie. No coat or jumper as it was warm out west.

    They also supplied me with a set of 'black and whites', black trousers, white religious style shirts with curved collars, black shoes and black socks. Also supplied was a long black soutane and white surplice which were worn at chapel. Also included were: all meals, transport to and from school in the tangerine Torana, accommodation and a $5.00 weekly spending allowance for train fares or other requirements. I was to collect the five dollars from Br Maurice the Bursar on the weekend or Monday morning and I gave him the change from the previous week. He said I could keep the 21 cents or 30 cents and that made the accounting easier. I didn't need to use my personal savings which I had made during my working life but I knew that once I was a permanent or fully Professed member of the Society all my cash would be handed over to them and my Will was to be in their favour. One might have said it was all laid on for me. I had no expenses and would be cared for in sickness and health for the rest of my life. All I had to do was live as a brother under the direction of the Superiors and the Rule of the Society, to pray and live a good life, to attend to academic study and basically be a good person.

During my first few weeks at Kemps Creek, I got to meet many of the others, however some seemed more recluse or happy with established circles of friends and people to hang out with, such as the four or five who often played canaster or some card game during which a player called out open or lay down misère or similar. They had a few buttons open on their white shirts revealing some pale chests. Others were busy with university study, others were high school teachers at St Simon Stock, Greystanes which had recently been given into the care of the SSG. Others were on the Motor Missions led by Br Maurice. They would drive around the western suburbs dropping off and picking up SRE teachers or 'Catechists' who taught religion in the local State schools. They often returned home tired and excited as well. That was the central mission of the Society founded by Brother John in the late 1950s. Maurice had been by his side from the early 1960s. The man I thought was a gardener was Brother Mark who was a senior Brother and a printer by trade. He used a special typewriter and ran the printer from a room in the house.

The teachers at Simon Stock included Br Joseph the Principal, Br Andrew and two others. I would travel with them packed into the Torana listening to the current affairs program 'AM' on the ABC as we zipped along the M4 and Parramatta Road. We left home immediately after morning prayer and a quick breakfast. They would drop me off at Westmead in the mornings and I'd get to them by train and a mile walk up along Ettalong Road in the afternoon. I'd attempt to do my homework at the teachers' desk in the staff room while waiting for them to return home for dinner and evening prayers.

    On Tuesdays I had an early mark and often called home to speak with mum from the public phone at Pendle Hill station. It was always good to talk with her and hear the family and parish news. My younger sister, Anne, was only 8 at the time and in primary school. Cathy and Peter were in early high school. Dad was a butcher at Kingsford on ANZAC Pde. All that year I never had a chance to visit them except for one weekend in January to participate in a CYO play for which I had practiced over several months. I played the part of Pontius Pilot (who flew in from the Middle East!). The brothers didn't have free access to vehicles and there were no buses to the St Marys train station which was a good ten to fifteen minutes' drive distant. We didn't have family visitors at all that I remember. Mrs Sweeney did pop in once a month with a huge suitcase or two packed with her son's washing. He had two sets, one being washed and ironed, one in the wardrobe or washing basket. Brother John didn't use the common washing machines preferring his mother to do it for him. She saw it as an honour and service to the Society and was president of the women's auxiliary for the Society of St Gerard, a fund-raising group. A few special guests appeared from time to time but they usually didn't dine with us or ate before or after our community meal. One group I remember called themselves something like The Family. Brother John briefly introduced them to us as they passed by on the grand tour of the monastery. He said they were sharing ideas regarding leadership and formation. I thought they were some sort of Cult group with wacky ideas about shared community activities including group love. We were never told much more about them, though they looked to me like hippies. Perhaps it's something I heard on the news or read in the Sun Newspaper on the way home from work in the city. Anyhow, the monastery was isolated from the outside community.

    One high profile visitor was Miles McKeon Bishop of Bunbury WA. I never forget the morning he was due to arrive. Brother Stephen Robinson got me cleaning fly spots off the yellow walls in his corridor as the bishop was to stay there for a few nights. I asked Stephen as I was up the ladder what I would say to the bishop if he walked by. I was to say "Good afternoon My Lord" and he would just see us doing usual Saturday house work, though that was not usual at all. Brother Stephen liked a bit of pretence rather than open transparency which would have been too awkward or perhaps embarrassing. The bishop was, apparently, a regular visitor and the brothers were invited to set up a community in his town. The Bishop had a Bishops' ring as all bishops had but his was that of the SSG, gold with the logo of Heart Speaks to Heart on it. The Society had a Bishop as an honorary member! So impressive.

    Later that year we all assembled together down at Bowral in the brothers' property Hopewood House. The acreage and huge mansion had been donated to the Society for their use. It contained the mansion, some sheds and garages and a large long worker's quarters in which certain Brothers stayed including Br John Sweeney, Joseph Pritchard and Stephen Robinson. I think some including the card players were down there too. Most of us were housed in the rooms and corridors and along the upper verandas of the old Hopewood House. We had 24-hour 'adoration' in the chapel and took turns to kneel and pray for an hour at half hourly intervals. Sometimes we had a 3 am shift or an afternoon shift so there was constant movement around the buildings at any half hour as we had to call or wake the man after us plus one. If my shift finished at 4am I'd wake the man on the 4:30 roster and so on. Stephen Robinson always seemed to be around in the midnight hours sitting at the rear of the chapel.

Once I asked others if I should or needed to visit Stephen or others in the secluded hall at the rear. I was told that it was not required to go and some even said it's like invitation only and if I was invited, I would know. One said: "Paul, you wouldn't want to go down there", without further clarification. It remained a mystery to me what went on in that hall. Perhaps I'd be honoured to discover next year on the feast of St Gerard, the 16th of October.

At that time some women were welcomed into the Society of St Gerard and Margaret Coffee and another received habits as Novices to become the Sisters of St Gerard. This was possible due to Rome recognising the Constitutions of the Society. The sisters moved into a cottage in western Sydney not far from the school grounds. I remember helping them move in and being offered cold coffee as they hadn't had the electricity connected. Also, at Bowral that weekend some of the senior Brothers made their final or perpetual vows after being in temporary vows for years. They received gold rings like the Bishop wore. The society of St Gerard Majella had become official on my 19th Birthday. Few remembered my celebration.

Meanwhile, earlier in the year I was assigned to a formation group with the teenagers and Brother Mark. We talked about the work of the Society and life rules around the house and learnt who was who in the hierarchy and we had to study the

Constitution of the Society and the meaning of Heart speaks to Heart. After a few weeks Brother Stephen walked into the group and spoke to Mark and I was to be exclusively in the care of Stephen Robinson who was also the Novice Master. I felt honoured by this promotion and special attention of Stephen. He was a tall man with thick dark hair and long hands, he played the chapel organ like it was a grand pipe organ of a Town Hall. Stephen Robinson and Lawrence Cross had produced a cassette of church songs and hymns including the Mass for Moderns which most Sydney churches used on Sundays. It was pumped out on the St Mary's Cathedral organ too. To have him as my mentor and spiritual guide was fantastic. I felt honoured, the Novice Master and a senior consultor to Brother John! The weekly guidance sessions were in his private room which had a desk near the door, a wardrobe at the far end and a single bed under the window with an unobscured view of back paddocks. His room was past the printery and Br Mark's room but before Maurice's room. Andrew stayed at the end of the yellow corridor and a few others slept along there too. Stephen explained after my first visit sitting at his desk that he had a bad back and needed to retire to bed early after dinner and he usually spoke to others while he lay in bed and the visitor would sit on the edge. I had nothing to say as he was the Brother Superior of the House and was not to be questioned. There was usually one young man in the room, one sitting on the floor outside and another waiting to see him. He was very popular amongst the brothers as a mentor and guide. He was only in his 30s at the time but very wise and charismatic.

During one of the guidance and information sessions with Stephen Robinson, he told me that he wished he was a priest so he could hear my confession. He said that the plan for the future was that some of the leading Brothers would go to Seminary and study for the Priesthood. The first would be Brother John who was at that time undertaking an abridged fast track program at the National Seminary at Kensington. Once several brothers were ordained, they wouldn't need outside visiting priests to come for Mass / Eucharist or other Liturgies and sacraments including Confession. They would hear each other's' confessions within the home communities. In the future they may have authority from the Bishop to run a parish too. Later that year Brother John was installed by the Bishop as an Acolyte and was able to minister Communion with the Chaplain.

On several occasions Brother Stephen singled me out to accompany him to fund raising events and when the brothers went to hear Handel's Messiah at Sydney Town Hall, he insisted I sit on his right side so he could whisper and explain all the music and theatre to me personally. I would do whatever he wished as he had complete control over my life, my education, what I wore and ate and where I sat in chapel which was just in front of his organ next to Brother Christopher. Brother Lawrence Cross had his room next to the chapel away from the other senior brothers in the upper wing. I asked him why he had a room there and not near the others. Curiously he told me he was happy to be there and not part of what they did up there. I didn't understand at all but was sure he had close access to the chapel for his love of Liturgy and Gregorian chant.

    One day on the way to school I was sitting in the front passenger seat listening to Suzie Quatro 'Can the Can' or '48 Crash' when I heard Brother Andrew from the back ask "Brother Paul, don't you have school today?" I said I did and asked why. He seemed most uneasy pointing out I still had my black and whites on not my grey uniform. Panic seemed to grip the car as we hurtled on to the school. I was taken into the staff room rather than being dropped off at my school. They feverously searched for a large jumper to cover my white shirt despite it being summer. I had to cover up lest other students and teachers at Parramatta Marist discovered I was a Brother of St Gerard. How embarrassing, I felt for them. I didn't understand the need for cover up or panic. I wore my home uniform into class. Others did ask and I had to tell them I lived with the brothers at Kemps Creek and that's what I wore at home. From that time, I was given special permission to wear my school uniform to chapel and breakfast! Special treatment but required.

Life went on that year, week after week month after month and season after season. School and home duties such as mowing the grass or doing my washing and ironing. At Christmas time I was allowed home to celebrate with my family and in my home parish where I was treated as some sort of celebrity. Even my grandfather called me Brother Paul.

After Christmas and towards the middle of January I received a phone call at home from Brother John himself. His booming voice of authority reached down the line all the way from western Sydney to sunny seaside Matraville right into my living room. He asked if I were returning and entering the Novitiate. I said I wasn't sure and was waiting for him to invite me. He said it's up to me to seek entry to the Novitiate. He continued without giving me time to think or respond: "If you aren't sure, just return here and pack your bags tomorrow. The novitiate program has been on hold waiting for you Paul." Yes, Brother I said with some sadness and sense of dismay. I took the bus and train out there and was collected at the station as before but by Stephen Robinson. I had ten minutes or so to pack my stuff into a bag. It had been piled into a corner already. The back room had been cleaned out and was to be a library and study area. I didn't have a chance to say goodbye to others. Stephen bundled me into the car and drove me home to Matraville where I was left in some bewilderment.

Once again, I was home with my parents and family, with no job, no future, unemployed and feeling lost and somewhat neglected by those who had promised to care for me for ever. The previous twelve months as a young Brother had suddenly come to a screeching halt as if a train had derailed at the beginning of a long-expected journey.

Chapter 3
Life in the 1970s

My family accepted me and welcomed me back home, I rocked up to the old CYO on Wednesday nights and Saturday afternoons and even volunteered to open the hall on Monday nights. I was elected onto the CYO Executive committee as a social member, then as a Vice President in later years I was also the Treasurer. I continued to attend church and later that year, 1974, I was elected onto the Parish Council as the Youth Representative. People asked why I had returned home, and I said it wasn't for me. I said I was happy to be home in Matraville again. No further questions.

As part of my job seeking strategy, I sat the Australian Public service entrance examination along with hundreds of others in a huge hall of the University of NSW in Kensington. It consisted of about ten pages of multiple-choice questions to be answered on a computerised booklet by filling in spaces with a led pencil. I received a letter thanking me for attending and that I would receive further notification when my application was successful. I was reminded that there were few spaces and that thousands applied.

In the meantime, I found work as a clerk in a warehouse at Botany and began to save money once again. The supermarket warehouse had a small admin office above the main warehouse, and I worked in the Gate House with a woman, Gladys, who had been there for years. My job was very methodical and systematic. I had to walk the aisles and collect completed computer printouts of goods which had been picked and loaded onto pallets for delivery to supermarkets across Sydney and the State as far as Orange, Dubbo, Blayney and Broken Hill and Bourke in far western NSW near the border with South Australia. Once a complete set of printouts were collected, I'd separate the three copies, one for the warehouse, one for the driver and one for the store. I had to wear a shirt and tie but they got stained every day with carbon. Gladys wore a work apron to protect her clothing. We finished at 3:30 and a night shift man began at 3:00 to take over till 9pm. There was a sandwich shop nearby where I got lunch. I never wanted to eat at my desk, something I had learnt to avoid during my time at the PMG. I needed a break from the desk at mealtime. Some of the packers invited me to sit with them at tea break and at lunch time so I joined them. We sat on packing cases and talked about life in Australia as many of them were new Australians. One day Mr Montgomery was walking through the warehouse and saw me talking with the packers. He called me aside and told me I shouldn't talk with them. I said it's only during break time thinking he thought I was slacking off. He said no. Not at any time should I talk with them unless to do with work, because they are packers and we are clerks. He said I wear a tie and work in an office, but they don't. I told my friends what the Warehouse manager said, and we laughed together. From then on someone was a lookout and warned me if the man in the tie was approaching. One-week Gladys was off, and I had to work extra hard till 6pm to get the work done. I put in for and got overtime pay. Soon the night shift man had holidays and I had to work till 9pm six days a week. I was raking in the money but had no social life. Dad would pick me up each night and I'd fall asleep immediately due to mental exhaustion from sorting all those papers all day. After three weeks of this I decided to call it quits and handed in my resignation to Mr Montgomery. At the end of the week, I went upstairs to pick up my pay, so I waited in the pay office for my name to be called. The paymaster sat in a cage behind security glass from which he called: "Ward, P." So, I fronted the window. He said no I'm looking for Ward P. I said that's me, Paul Ward. Oh, he said apologising. "I've been paying you 10% less than you should have received." I must have looked puzzled, so he explained I had been on female rates. He asked if I would return the next week to collect the back pay. The next week I entered via the usual back gate and saw dear old Mr Montgomery sitting at my old desk sorting the papers and getting carbon on his white shirt and blue tie. I smiled to myself as I collected my back pay and took the bus home.

  I was soon looking for another job. Banking. I was to work in banking but as a teller. Who doesn't like handling money? I can count money already I thought, and I like people and it's a neat and tidy looking workplace too. ANZ bank here I come!

  Why the ANZ? The Commonwealth was too big and official looking. The Commercial Bank was too much into business – Commercial. The Rural Bank seemed to be associated with the countryside and farmers, so I wondered why it was in the city suburbs. That seemed wrong to me for a rural bank to be in the city. Besides, when I was a primary school, I won a prize for musical composition and my three lines of music was displayed in the window of the local Rural Bank however I never got my original work back. So, I was anti Rural Bank. The ANZ theme colour was light blue, it looked friendly and included New Zealand an island nation off the Australian coast. Therefore, based on all these facts and opinions and youthful impressions I answered an ad to work for the ANZ.

My first appointment was to a small branch in the busy 'dormitory suburb' of Randwick. Randwick was packed full of university students who studied at the University of New South Wales, uphill from Randwick racecourse, Randwick TAFE and famous Coogee beach lay downhill to the east. A strip of shops ran along the main road including other banks, real estate agents, solicitors, doctors, chemists, a fruit shop and a few cafes and 'fast food' outlets. Colonel Sanders' Kentucky Fried Chicken (KFC) was one of them I frequented during my 30-minute lunch breaks. The lunch box was my favourite, with three pieces of chicken, hot mashed potato with gravy, a bun, a tub of coleslaw and a serving of French fries with a can of drink, usually Pepsi cola. KFC was across the road and two blocks up from the bank. I usually had to wait a while and got back to the lunchroom upstairs with five minutes to spare during which I consumed the meal, washed up and was ready to return for the afternoon session downstairs.

Being fresh into banking my job there was 'batching clerk'. I would collect vouchers and documents from each teller and stamp them with the date and bank branch stamp and bundle them into batches for processing in the city over night. Not a high security job. I wasn't handling cash, just vouchers and elastic bands and rubber stamps. An hour or so a day I would be found in the corner updating the 'Standing Orders' folder which hadn't been updated for years. I worked methodically and chronologically from the oldest updates to the latest, often changing regulations of the same chapter a few times a week as I worked my way through. It was like sections A - K, A paragraph 1, sub- paragraphs ii to xv and so on. I loved that job.

At the end of my first week the pay cheques were issued by the accountant. Each teller and clerk were paid, but I missed out. My name had not yet appeared on the list of employees. Being a good young man, just 19 or so, I said it was ok, they could pay me the following week. Oh no, the union rep and others cried. Paul must be paid today. So, the Accountant took a guess and wrote out a bank cheque to the value of a neat $100.00 saying if it was too much or too little, we would fix it up later. That was the very first time I had seen a cheque for one hundred dollars or been paid so much money. Banking, oh I was enjoying it.

My second week in banking at Randwick was to be one of the most memorable and exciting highlights of my life.

One hot sunny afternoon as I was heading out to lunch, a foreign looking woman wearing a scarf and bright dress and polished shoes, strolled into the bank. I remember holding the door open for her as she was carrying a large paper bag. Off I went to order my favourite KFC lunch. After a while I became aware of voices calling my name. Thinking there must be other men in the street called Paul, I took no notice. I knew no one in Randwick therefore never thought it was me being called. The accountant himself was out looking for me. I was needed back at the bank. I was told to bring my lunch and run. That sort of thing I find so frustrating. I had my allotted time for lunch. Also, I was a junior staff member and knew of no urgent reason I would be required in a rush. As he was my boss and a very kind man and I had my lunch in my hot hand I headed back, under some duress. I didn't like missing out on mealtime and being a person with Asperger's (not that I knew so then) I really hated having my routine broken unexpectedly. I tried to at least eat the chicken and had to leave the remainder in the lunchroom fridge.

All male bank employees, including myself, had to wear a tie at work and had to arrive and leave in a suit coat. Clothing regulations! I was asked to put on my coat and go outside and hail a taxi and ask the driver to wait till we were ready. Ready for what I wondered, standing there in the hot sun in my coat and tie. With the taxi waiting I was summonsed inside again and asked to go to the manager's office where I saw heaps of foreign currency in neat piles on the manager's desk. The foreign French speaking woman had arrived direct from New Caledonia with a bag full of French Francs, got off the plane at Sydney airport that morning and travelled the short distance to our branch with her bag of cash. It turned out to be over 100,000 francs in cold hard cash. At the manager's desk I was asked if I was over 18. Yes, I said. 'Ok,' the accountant requested 'Paul, please sign on the dotted line for this gun.' I signed for a lump of metal, apparently a six-shooter revolver of some kind. I was told not to shoot at anyone, but to shoot into the air if required. My clammy hands took the gun and I was told to put it in my coat pocket within easy reach. I was to sit in the back of the taxi with the gun for security, while the accountant was to sit in the front with the cash in one of those linen bank bags hidden in his now bulging briefcase. The taxi driver was not to know of the cargo, and he was to drive us by the most direct route to the ANZ branch of King and Pitt streets in the city. The gun pressed against my chest from under the seat belt which crossed over from right to left anchored in at my left thigh. My heart thumped on the left and the gun pressed on the right. My mind was wondering what to do in case we were held up. Held up in traffic was time enough for panic as anyone could force the cab door open, reach in for the cash bag and I would have to fight them off with the six-shooter gun. What if some dirty rotten thief saw what had transpired on the main road of Randwick? What if the woman had been followed from the airport? What if she was a French secret agent or a spy? I loved James Bond movies and though she may have been a Bond girl or worse, a KGB undercover woman trading in laundered money at an unsuspecting local bank branch! What if that man in the car in the next lane at the stop lights noticed the bulge in my coat pocket, guessed it was a gun, guessed I was an inexperienced bank security guard, that there was cash in the taxi cab and jumped out, grabbed my gun, held it to my head and stole the cash from the accountant? I'd be in trouble then, I thought. I was supposed to guard the cash, not have my gun stolen along with the 100,000 French francs. I felt mighty responsible for that cash, the life of the accountant and not to mention the taxi driver who probably had a wife and family waiting for him to return home safely without a bullet hole in his body, or worse. My parents would be waiting for me to return home for dinner of lamb chops, mashed potatoes peas and beans with mint sauce after my boring day batching vouchers at the bank. Who would break the news to them that I was in hospital with a bullet wound to my arm and face? Would my dinner be wasted? Probably not, my brother Peter would eat it. What about the KFC in the fridge, would that be wasted? We were taught at school never to waste food and think of the poor people of Biafra. I made sure the taxi door was locked and tried to look calm as if this was a normal part of my day guarding a sack full of foreign currency with a six shooter in my coat pocket pressed against my chest. To the left we turned, down Alison Road, past the racecourse, past the TAFE, stopped at the lights on ANZAC Parade for ages, turning right into ANZAC Pde., through into Taylors' Square, one of the busiest intersections in Sydney. Crawling through the traffic, every stop, every pedestrian every car was noted in case I had to write a report. Down Liverpool street, past Hyde Park turning into Elizabeth Street past the double decker buses. Who could see in and notice what was going on? Who was that innocently dashing across from the park in front of our car? Turning into King Street having passed Martin Plaza, which was teaming with shoppers, women with prams, men with coats, youths, and all kinds traversed Martin Plaza. King Street led down to Pitt and we parked in the street outside the bank. The accountant had to pay the driver while I wondered what to do next being aware, we were out on the public streets of Sydney. Eventually we strode across the road through the revolving doors and into the cool banking chamber of head office. They were expecting us both and we were ushered into an office behind the teller's counter and the cash was counted and checked by local staff. As I declined to take the gun home to mum's place (which I realise now was never going to happen, one of the accountant's dry jokes.) We caught another taxi back to Randwick where the office had closed as by now it was after 3pm. The accountant opened the door, put the alarm off and I signed the six-shooter back into his care and placed it securely in the manager's safe.

    Mum was wondering where I was as I turned up later than usual. She didn't get the full story and no gun was mentioned. Not something you tell your mother who jumps at the sound of a bird in the tree outside. Many topics were off limits in our 1970s Catholic household: sex and drugs and wild parties were amongst them; I guessed the story of their young curly haired son carrying a six shooter through Sydney streets was one of those off-limit topics.

    The next week I was then sent off to the Tellers' Training School for two weeks. Four or five of us young lads learnt how to count money, take deposits and write the information in customers' bank books. We learnt about cheques and heard about telegraphic transfers but didn't need to know about them as the accountant would process transactions like those. We also learnt how to describe bank robbers by height, estimate their weight, colour of clothes and so on. Secret cameras and guns were fascinating for this young teenager too. Please don't say the bank had no computers. Oh, they had one in the city office which sorted the cheques, a Magnetic Ink Character Recognition (MICR) machine. And another one or two which computed the daily cash in and cash out of each teller at each branch. This was so that if any money didn't balance on the rare occasion a teller made an error, it could all be checked and fixed up. We trainees were also told that any money we 'lost' had to be made up by ourselves, the tellers. What happened to any money 'over'? The bank got that, not the teller! Simple.

In a bedazzled state of mind with new information swirling about and me trying to make sense of what I had 'learnt' in a ten-day crash course, I was informed by head office that from the next Monday I was to report for work at the Rosebery branch on dusty Gardeners Road under the flight path of the 747s heading to and from Sydney AirPort at suburban Mascot only a few kilometres away. I happily told my family and checked out the local area for bus stops, lunch shops and all that. Orientation done I bought a few new ties and fresh shirts for my new job. Word went around the family and neighbourhood that after a few years of moving from job to job and going back to school and then out again, Paul had landed a permanent position as a bank teller. Things could only look up from there.

Arriving early on the Monday I waited nervously outside for the other staff to arrive and open up. We started at 9 for an opening at 10 but most were in the office and on duty before then. I was greeted by the others and introduced around the branch. There were the manager Mr Betts, the accountant Mr Worthington, two other tellers a young man Bruce and a mature woman who would have been going on 30 by the name of Beryl. Then there were the office girls Jan and Millie. I was shown the security arrangements, the camera triggers, signed for a six shooter with five bullets in it, signed for something like $20,000 in notes and coin and shown my tellers' box. I was to be number one teller once the doors opened for business! I was fresh out of Teller Training and knew all there was to know about banking in the 1970s, that's why the merely 20yr old got the top spot.

Longingly I glanced across at the enquiry counter or across at the quiet end where number 3 stood waiting for customers to deposit their pension cheque and withdraw $20 for the week. I was getting paid $100 a week before tax, to serve business customers and their multi thousand-dollar transactions, hold a gun under the counter, and keep track of scores of transactions a day, including the pensioner lady who wanted to chat and asked me to mind her house keys while she went shopping. Debits on one side, credits on the other, anxious customers lining up in front of me, recording it all by hand in ink on vouchers and counting every cent twice. There was no time for double checking and counting. If I couldn't trust a bank customer, who could I? Wrong thinking Paul. Trust no one. But did I really have to check and mark things off as I went along? Couldn't I just do it at the end of the day? Days and weeks came and went. Each Friday we would head down to the pub on the corner of Botany and Gardeners roads for a beer. Beryl was first down there and saved a table. I was often late. I'll never forget Beryl saying the first one never touched the sides. She was a woman who could down a schooner of beer in one mouthful. I drank middies even though the others may have thought I was weak. I was going out with my mates from the CYO, the local catholic church youth group and I had to be home in time to change and get out again. Those were the days young people went out at 7.30 and were home by 1am at the very latest. I'd often decline Friday drinks so that I could just get on the bus home. I was also usually late counting the money.

    Tellers had to balance their bookwork and cash to the last cent each and every day. The other two balanced within 10 minutes of closing and got on with other work or dashed off home. I took at least half an hour on a good day with the accountant waiting for me to finish and lock my gun and cash in the safe. A little trick was to have an 'under' and overs' tin on the shelf under the counter, just next to the gun. This tin was unofficial, but every good teller had one. The tin contained loose coins up to about a dollar or two. Remember, in the case the teller was under, cash was put in from their own pocket to make it balance but if the cash was 'over' that meant a customer was short money so the bank kept it till someone could prove it was theirs. No one ever did though.

Teller number one at the ANZ Rosebery branch balanced every day. Ok, would you believe most days and then only had to put in a few cents? Would you believe he would have to put in a few dollars on occasion? Truth be told, the 'number one' balanced twice in six months. Two times. A party was held in the pub when I balanced my books. We rarely had such parties.

Australian bank notes were colour coded, brown for one-dollar notes, green and gold for the twos, purple for the fives and green and blue for tens with red for twenties. There were no fifties or hundreds in the 70s. Coins were 1c, 2c, 5c, 10c, 20c and the octagonal 50 cent coin. Notes were counted and bundled in little heaps of 10 notes of each denomination, so a fold of $1.00 notes was $10 and a bundle was $100 of one-dollar notes. On to a fold of $10 notes being $100 and a bundle of $10 being $1000. So, a fold of $20s was

$200 while a bundle of $20s was $2000. The coin was rolled in paper with the 1c in 50cent rolls, 2c in $2 rolls and so on according to the size or value or whatever fitted evenly into the printed coin wrappers.

Coin scales or note counters were not known of in suburban branches. It was all done by hand. One day I had to count a bag of loose 20cent coins, a thousand dollars of the stuff and roll it in paper. Someone had apparently ordered bulk coin rather than rolled coin from the reserve bank. That all being totally clear and I ever so calm and focussed and unfazed it was a breeze to balance my $40,000 cash to the last cent daily! Really? Not.

Pay clerks would come in on Thursdays or Fridays which was the busiest day for the number one teller. Blue collar workers were paid cash in pay-envelopes which contained their weekly or fortnightly income down to the cent. These pay clerks were very efficient and I had to give them what they needed in change. They couldn't just take 10s and 20s and off they went. It was the whole range of notes and coin needed to pay each of their team of factory workers correctly. They would bring in a cheque and get thousands of dollars cash in various denominations. I'd be handing over folds of $1 notes, and bundles of fives, tens and twenties. Each fold and bundle had to be counted. 10, 20, 30, 40, 50, 60, 70, 80, 90,

100 X 10 = $1000.00 and the same but twice the value with the $20 notes. Then I'd had over bundles counting, one thousand, two thousand, and sometimes several bundles of 10s or 20s. The pay clerk didn't want to go back short of cash or with the wrong combinations, so he checked as I went along. It was always correct due to the double checking on both sides of the counter. I never had to worry about the big cash deals, it was always the small ones of a few dollars or cents which caught me up and made me not balance each day.

Then one Friday I was balancing and looking forward to a relaxing weekend when it was discovered that I was 'under' by $2000!! Two thousand dollars! All the money in the safe was checked by each teller. Eventually Mr Worthington said to go home and not to worry as it was probably on paper and as usual the computer check would locate the error and it would all be sweet by 8am Monday. I must have looked more stressed than usual over the weekend but never told anyone as I was sure it would be an error on paper. Monday morning and I arrived early to find the accountant pouring over the printouts and reports. My bookkeeping had been correct that day, but I was still short by $2000.

As I say, my pay was only $100 a week, and I had saved almost $1000. Paying back $2000 would take ages. I was told that in the event it did not turn up I could not pay it off weekly or monthly I had to come up with the total, but they would give me a fortnight to pay it back. I paid extra attention that day. Then on the stroke of 5 to 4 the last customer walks in, waits his turn for me and puts a brown paper bag on my counter saying, 'I think you may have been looking for this, Paul'. There was the missing $2000 cash! I thanked him very much. However according to the bank records, I was 'over' by $2000 that day. The manager and accountant kindly balanced it off for me. Down at the pub the first one didn't touch the sides that day, even though it was a Monday. Saved!

Spoiled notes were another feature of banking in an industrial area of Sydney. Occasionally someone would come in with a partial bank note and we would send it off to head office who would measure it and say the note is worth 60% or 45% or whatever. Some notes were torn as they were paper back then. One day a regular customer walks in with a sheepish grin all over his face. He worked at a commercial printing factory. They printed magazines like Dolly or Cleo or Women's Day. He had a heap of un-counted mixed notes which had been grabbed from a vat of spilt ink. Who knows how the notes got into the ink? They felt greasy and were all different colours of the rainbow and some colours I had not imagined before in my life. I counted them with the accountant at my side. They all had to go to the Reserve

Bank for checking and we'd get back to them. It was all ok in the end, but they had to wait weeks for the reply. The notes had to be checked for forgeries and all that.

As usual I was working late on a Friday when one of the senior male clerks told me to expect a blond woman to come knocking at the door and to let her in. He had arrived that morning with a holiday bag saying he was going camping for the weekend. The blond turned up, asked for John and I let her in. They kissed and hugged and went out the back door off for their weekend. Shortly later the phone rang but I ignored it as we had closed for the weekend. It rang again so I answered it thinking it may be urgent. A lady asked for John. I said he had gone for the weekend, and that his wife came, and they went out together. The woman on the phone quivered "I am, his wife!" and hung up.

The next Monday I was taken aside by an embarrassed but surprisingly calm John who said I was never to make assumptions about others and their relationships. I was not in the good books, but he was gracious saying I was not to know, and he should have told me it was another woman and not to say anything if someone called.

Carrying a loaded gun through the city streets, losing $2000 or dobbing a husband into a wife, I'm not sure which was more exciting working for the ANZ bank. However, more drama was to come.

Five or six months after I had joined Rosebery branch our good Mr Worthington went on annual leave and Mr Betts had been transferred to a regional office. The new manager left everything to the accountant and usually left work early. I think he was just seat warming till something more interesting came along. The acting accountant was, shall I say, meticulous. He was tall and broad in stature and very sure of himself and took no half measures. Not the man to be messed with. He took no sides, didn't go to the pub with the others, he was very straight up and down. Also, I thought he was not the type to be met in a dark alley of a night, if you know what I mean. He would have been a tough bouncer at a pub in Kings Cross, so I imagined. Not that I had been to The Cross myself. It had a reputation I chose not to experience. Thugs and drug dealers hung out at the Cross. Not that he would have been a drug dealer but I would not have wanted to blink in the wrong direction with this man around.

  Yet another Friday afternoon he stayed behind while I balanced my cash as usual. I could hear him huffing and puffing in his office. I could feel him breathing down my neck and the hairs on my arms were electric with tension. He came into my teller's box closed the door behind him and stood there watching every move, every blink of an eye, every stroke of my pen. I managed to balance.

Relief! I could lock up and go. Not in such a rush young man. What's this tin under the counter next to your gun? Oh, just the 'under and overs' tin I honestly replied. I said it's not part of my cash. He said whatever is in this teller's box, in the cash drawer or in a tin was to be counted. I was found to be 92 cents over that day.

    I was then ordered to open my box in the safe which was locked with two keys. I complained bravely saying I had not accessed that reserve all day and he knew it. He held the second key but had unlocked his side so that the number one teller didn't have to bother him for the key during a busy day. He stood by me almost leaning on my shoulder as I stood there and unfolded each bundle, each fold of notes and counted them freshly, twice. I was in tears and quaking in my boots by this stage of the stand-over bully tactics. He insisted it was his job to make sure all the cash in the branch was counted, correct, balanced and secure. And so, it was.

    The next week all was quiet till I was called into the acting accountants' office and asked to take a seat. I wondered if others had spoken to him and he was going to apologise for his heavy-handed approach as he had appeared happy all day. He presented me with a typed letter. Wow I thought, he has apologised in writing and put it in a sealed envelope. He said the letter was from head office in Sydney. I was to read it and reply immediately. Wow I thought, head office has apologised on his behalf. Someone had spoken up for me, perhaps it was Beryl and if so, I'd shout her a beer or two. I opened the envelope, took out the letter, and unfolded it with the official ANZ logo on the top. It was short. "It would be appreciated if Mr Ward would tender his resignation." Very short and direct. No need to waste ink on that. Pools of sweat formed under my hands and beads of the salty substance rolled down the back of my neck. I had never in my life been asked to resign. Never. Noticing, as a person with Asperger's often does, that the wording was 'it would be appreciated if...' I cottoned on to those words of hope asking this neatly dressed brute of a man from which testosterone oozed with every breath from every pore of his body: 'what if I don't resign?' The brute was slightly amused and ever so slightly put off guard. 'What do you mean Paul?' I replied brazenly that the letter was not one of sacking me, rather asking me to resign. So, sir, what if I refused to resign as they appreciated I might?' He was quick off the mark now having had time to consider his situation. 'Have you ever been to Bourke, Paul?' I knew it was over but gave it my next shot. 'No?' I enquired. He said that he could transfer me to the Bourke branch starting next week if I chose to stay with the bank. Bourke is the town in Australia the back of which is 'the back of beyond', the 'never-never'! The Australian Outback began at the back of Bourke. It is on the edge of the desert; temperatures are up to 40 Celsius of a day and cold of a night with desert dust storms blowing around the town and wild dingoes roaming after dark. Women of that town locked themselves in doors in Bourke and only ventured out in daylight hours. It was a hot stinky place no man in his right mind would visit, let alone work there. Unless they were either as tough as the thug opposite me or unless he sent you there. Ok I said. I wrote on a blank paper soon soaked in my perspiration: Dear ANZ bank. I resign today. Paul Ward. The thug took it, stamped it with the official branch date stamp and smiled as I trod out with my bag over my shoulder to be alone and dazed on Gardeners Road aimlessly looking for a bus, any bus, to get me out of there as soon as possible.

The next Monday I slept in. Mum came to my door asking if I was well and should they call the bank. No, I said, I'm ok. Its Monday Paul, why aren't you going to work? I got the sack mum. I don't have a job. Mum went into see dad who was just about to leave too. She told him that Paul says he isn't going to work because he got the sack from the bank. Dad appeared with a gravely serious face. What's that you told your mother, son? When dad calls me 'son' it's serious. So, I told him about the letter from head office and the chance I turned down of working in Bourke on the edge of the great Australian outback.

I said it's ok though. I have a new job starting on Wednesday, with the Public Service in the city. That past Friday I had received a second letter much different from the earlier one. In it the Public Service Office in Sydney said that I had passed the recent assessment test and was invited to report in on Wednesday at 8.30am to an address in George Street.

Great relief all round. Paul had a new job, with the Public Service. A job for life.

Settled and moving.

That Wednesday morning, I turned up bright and early at the Australian Public Service office in the city and was called to be interviewed briefly by a woman in the office. She welcomed me and offered a few jobs in different Government Departments including Defence, the Postmaster General's and one other. I said I had been with the PMG before and asked for that job. When I arrived Mr. Kevin Ryan, was distracted as he thought I was just popping in to say hello to my former work mates. He said he was glad to see me, but he was waiting for a new recruit. I said that's me. I gave him my letter of introduction and he shook my hand with a warm welcome and took me to the admin Clerk to set me up with pay roll and all that stuff. I was given a job in the Money Order Inquiries section as a clerical assistant grade one. I was beginning at the bottom of the pecking order once again. The Public Service had a Seniority List which Kevin kept in his top drawer in a manila envelope. It was updated annually but he had a copy dating back several years too. There were two major strata of officers in the office: Clerical Assistants grades 1 to 5 and Clerks grades 1 to 5 or so. Then a select few were managers. A worker with the HSC began as a Clerk and was able to perform certain duties with steps of authority such as preparing Money Orders but then needing a higher Clerk to sign them. A Money Order is a value document purchased at a Post Office and, similar to a cheque, is used to send money to a payee who deposits it in their bank account. Once paid it is stored as evidence for two years. An employee such as myself without the HSC could only ever be a Clerical Assistant (C/A) beginning at Grade 1 which was basic sorting envelopes or counting papers or basic tasks. The only way a C/A could perform the duties of a Clerk was by the appointment of a senior manager and then only in an 'acting' role for a limited period replacing a Clerk who was on Leave. So, not only seniority but also separate levels dependant on education and experience. You couldn't go up the list unless a person at the top resigned or retired.

    Once or twice a year some old person would retire, or a woman would marry or have a baby. We would collect cash and buy a gift for them and they would be presented with something on Pay Day. Usually, retirees got a gold watch after their 40 years of service filing papers. When I had resigned a few years earlier they took up a collection and I bought a leather brief case valued at $35.00. For the pay day collections most of us put in 20c or up to one dollar. If we knew the person well over several years some would put in $5.00!

Our pay was delivered accompanied by an armed guard and our names were called out by the manager and cash envelopes were handed out by a Pay Clerk supervised by a colleague. I'd collect my few dollars and deposit it into the bank across the road. Some workers would make little heaps of cash for each of their household bills and expenses. I didn't bother. I just had enough to pay board to my parents and buy the weekly bus ticket for $3.50 and then buy lunch at the canteen on level 9 each day and the newspaper every morning. I'd spend a few dollars on the weekend for drinks and snacks at the discoes and some on smokes, not that I smoked a lot, two or three cigs a day. When I needed cash, I'd withdraw via my savings account book and take out $5 asking for two twos and a one. Remember my weekly ticket was $3.50, so a five-dollar withdrawal was something special.

I was often so bored and up to date with my work, I had time especially during tea breaks to explore around parts of the old GPO others never visited. Once I saw a door open and walked into some sort of secret and secure room which was airconditioned and had a raised floor. In the middle of the room on a long table were what appeared to be tapes going around at set intervals. I heard a recording similar to this: At the third stroke, it will be 3:45 and fifty seconds, dong, dong, dong. At the third stroke it will be 3:46 precisely, dong, dong, dong. It was my favourite talking clock which I used to call up and listen to as a boy. I used to go to the public phone on the corner and dial 1194 and get to listen to the voice of John Chance telling us the time. There I was in the electric clock room. No one saw me. I told no one. Now you know. What if I jumped and the clock skipped ten seconds?

I often had to take papers down to level five from seven and used the lift. They were all operated by a lift driver who had a seat near the door because they had some physical disability, probably from the War. We would tell them where we wanted to go and they would press the buttons and open and close two sets of doors. Some old lifts were operated by a leaver. The driver would swing the leaver to the left or right to drive the lift up or down. One of my all-time favourites was in the neighbouring building in Pitt Street, the John Sands Building which had some rarely visited offices and the ground floor Philatelic Bureau. That lift had a pully mechanism where the operator pulled down on a rope to raise the lift and up to pull it down. Sometimes I'd sneak in there just for fun. Another time I borrowed a lift! The lift man had popped into the gents for a moment, so I borrowed his lift. I swung the doors shut and moved the handle to go down. I delivered my papers and got back to drive myself up again. He was waiting for me outside and told me not to steal a lift again. I didn't but it was fun anyway. The secrets are out now.

    Apparently, my boss heard of me getting around the building and called me into his office. He said he understood I got bored and needed to walk around the building exploring places. I said yes but I only went during break times. He said that's ok but from now on if I go around the GPO, I should carry a piece of paper and a pen so that I look as if I'm doing something or going somewhere. I agreed though I thought it was a bit silly to carry a paper and pretend I was doing something. I had to look as if I was legitimate so no one would think I'm doing the wrong thing. Most people wouldn't go walking around just out of curiosity, I guess. Being the NSW State HQ of the Australian Post Office and the Telecommunications Office there were some sensitive offices in the building. Apparently, some days the Telecom staff received bomb threats such as: fix my phone or I'll bomb the office.

The threats had to be taken seriously but although they were on level three, we on levels five to seven weren't disturbed by evacuation orders!

After a while I was given different work to carry out including operating a computer called a MICR machine. Remember, the ANZ Bank had some in the city? The Australian Post Office had recently become Australia Post and the NSW office took over the processing of all Money Orders from across Australia. They were sorted and sent back to other capital city GPOs for storage. A MICR machine was housed in a special airconditioned room with a raised floor and dust proof conditions. We had to wear white dust coats in the room. The machine was vacuum cleaned each morning and had regular maintenance from the manufacturers, IBM. The MICR could read 1,500 documents a minute but one digit per pass so we had to sort the documents by five or six passes per day so that they were in order. There was the State field including State and Office or suburb code. The banks call this the BSB code. Once in that order they had to be sorted into numerical order from 000001 to 999999. One-digit line at a time. They were stored in cartons and those from interstate sent back. A few months later management decided that as Sydney had the sorting machine, we would keep all the documents there and staff from other state headquarters would call or write to us with any enquiries. My manager took me aside one afternoon and asked me if I could take control of the storage of the whole lot. He said I was doing a good job with the NSW set. I said yes, I could do it and he gave me a promotion to National Storage Officer, though still classed as a C/A. I had to calculate the physical requirements and internal logistics. Initially floor space was utilised in vast open spaces. Office staff, usually women had to kneel on the dirty floor to look for documents. I soon seconded spare odd rooms and the boss got steel filing cabinets. It soon became apparent that this ad hoc system was not enough, and I managed to get several women and key staff to petition the manager who saw the need and asked me to fix it. I was given some free reign and allowed to think out of the box. I said the ideal was one or two large storage spaces so that staff were not wasting time walking all over the place. The documents were to be stored for two years or more then destroyed. They had to be in a secure environment with a door locked after hours. I managed to get one large room of about 30 by 30 metres in size. Structural engineers were engaged to conduct floor stress tests and consulted me about shelving size and requirements. Another similar sized room was found in the Sub Basement for documents over 13 months old. I designed cardboard shoebox style cartons with a hinged lid so that five could fit on standard shelves. The shelving was two metres high with bays a metre wide and five shelves per bay and ten bays long across the room. The shelving was in rows back-to-back about ten deep. That's 20 sets of rows, fifty shelves per row, 20 cartons per shelf, up to 2000 items per carton. All sorted by date, by state, locality and numerical order. If someone asked for money orders paid at Maroubra on the 3rd of July 1976 or Darwin on the 19th of September 1977, I could direct them to the spot within a metre. The states had colour coded labels, white for NSW, red – Vic, Blue – Qld, Yellow – SA, Green – Tas and orange for WA. My brother Peter's workplace supplied the labels as he was a printer.

I remained in Australia Post for close on seven years as a clerical assistant and at times acting clerk. I really enjoyed being the storage officer. So much stability, sets of patterns, appropriate responsibility and so on.

Outside the stability

My private life, social and family and church carried on with some measure of fluidity balanced by the stability of Australia Post where my personnel file ran to several cards compared to some who had just one line for forty years' service.

Between 1970 and 1980 I had changed my home address several times. I lived at Matraville, Mittagong, Matraville again, Randwick – Cook Street, Randwick

- Alison Rd, Kensington, back to Alison Rd, Hillsdale, Matraville - Beauchamp Rd.

The Catholic church was one constant through all that including many years with the Matraville CYO from 1972, then 1974 - '79. Dad took me down one Wednesday night and left me in the car park of the church hall where I joined the CYO. I was rarely seen away from there for several years.

As a member of the CYO I held several positions on the leadership committee we called the executive. Over various years I was a social secretary, vice president, treasurer and secretary. I was never president, nor did I wish to be. We held Exec meetings fortnightly, usually on a Sunday night with fortnightly general meetings. The hall was open to members every Wednesday night and Saturdays. After a while I volunteered to open the hall on Mondays too. We'd plan outings for every weekend such as going to a disco, on a summer picnic, birthday parties, engagements or just coffee at the airport which was close by. A few times a year we'd go away for the weekend. Summertime it was usually camping or in holiday sheds and at the end of winter season, to the Snowy Mountains. Our Chaplain would accompany us on weekends away, that was Fr Ken Sargent we called him Sarg'. He was assistant priest at Matraville and was actually stationed there due to the location in close proximity to Kensington where he was a theological lecturer at St Paul's Seminary. He also trained SRE teachers or Catechises for the Archdiocese of Sydney.

    Eventually Fr Sargent was moved on to another parish and I took on the role of CYO liaison officer between the CYO executive and the Parish Priest who didn't attend meetings or gatherings due to his age and being busy otherwise. It was a tough period for me. I was the man in the middle. I had to listen to the desires of the club and the wishes and concerns of the Parish Priest. I had to be on both sides of the fence so to speak. My skills in negotiation were put to the test on many occasions. The first month we organised a CYO Saturday dance I had to ask the old PP, Fr Roche for permission to use the hall for the event. He approved but not till he asked me at his back door "What's the grog situation?" This was a very direct question, one to which I knew the answer but a question I had not anticipated. My initial thought was: 'Oh, bugger! The Parish Priest knows we have grog at the dances!' I next thought: I can't bluff or hide the facts. He knows somehow despite the extreme efforts to hide the signs.' We had taken pains to collect all evidence, wash the floor and empty bins. I had to be honest with the older and wiser more experienced man standing there at the screen door. Fr Roche was in his late 60s to early 70's I'd say. He had been a Chaplain on Australian Navy ships during the Second World War. He had suffered war, malaria, lost a lung due to smoking and had turned grey. He was well respected among his peers and organised the Sydney priest's tennis competition. He was thin, wiry, with tight short hair and a slightly drawn face covered in character marks. His beady blue eyes gazed with authority and trust. I had to be open and honest, representing the youth of the parish, being on the Parish Council and an active person in the parish. I wasn't a stranger asking for a hand out or a prayer. I was Paul Ward and he John Roche, we had a professional relationship and he was by far my senior. "The grog situation." - repeating these three words gave me a brief moment to consider my response. I had to be honest as well as cautious. "Yes Father, we were planning to sell some alcohol at the dance, it would be age restricted, however if you say so, we won't have it and I will pass on your ruling to the Executive and members. - We were in negotiation. - The wise old man had his opinion and response ready. He let it be known that he was disappointed that 'the grog situation' at our dances had not been honestly reported to him in the past. I just said "yes Father". The Parish Priest allowed grog at the dance under strict conditions that only those over 18 drank and that drinks were monitored to ensure no one got drunk. He said he had a duty of care to the young people of the parish and he was ultimately responsible. "Yes Father", I said. He was on the front foot in negotiations. What he decreed was the word. The priest continued that this would be the final time alcohol would be available at a CYO function, that it must be controlled and that no one was to smuggle in their own supplies or they would be asked to leave the dance. He suggested that he would select and appoint a couple of parishioners to visit the event during the night. I could see he was being generous and he would prefer there was no grog at the dances. I guessed he may personally visit for a walk through. I had to step up and speak clearly and diplomatically to the CYO leadership, the Executive. I knew certain members would complain but I also knew there was no further negotiation. It was tough but not as tough as was to transpire later the next year.

    Due to the shortage of Priests in the Church of Sydney the PP had to find another solution to the chaplaincy situation. He knew he was too old and set in his ways to be a realistic youth Chaplain and guide. A deacon from the Seminary was appointed to care for us on a casual and part time basis. It was to be part of his formation for ministry. A young man in his thirties was introduced to the parish as the CYO chaplain. He attended the executive and general meetings and visited on some Wednesday nights and Saturday mornings. He also went away with us for our annual trip to the Snowy Mountains on the October long weekend. Sorry but I forget his name. He was more relaxed than Fr Sargent and definitely more approachable than Fr Roche. He had a balance of being friendly but also firm and fair. Towards the end of 1979 came the annual elections for our exec team. It must have been exam time for the deacon or something and he was not present or we were between Chaplains. Whatever the case it was up to me to monitor the elections and report to the PP in real time. The procedure was as usual, for nominations for each position, they were to be screened by the Priest and voting would happen. Usually, several people were nominated for key roles such as Social Secretary, Treasurer and Vice President. A team of three including non-contenders supervised the counting and usually the winner was proclaimed and appointed automatically by the members present. This year, though, the PP wanted to be the final decision maker. He accepted the nominations for all but President. He insisted that at least the President was a practicing Catholic who would report to the PP and the Parish Council. None of the three names submitted were able to put their hand up and say they were practicing Catholics. For some it was a peer group 'look'. Some actually went to Sunday Mass most weekends; some took up the collection and others sang and played music in church. Sadly no one was able to commit in front of their peers or declined to run as

President. I was not prepared to run as CYO president either. Most of the others looked to me to stand as president, they all knew I was a devout catholic and was sure to be accepted by the Priest. I declined. The priest stood firm. No practicing catholic president, no CYO in the parish. His final word. I felt the group could still be a social group based around basketball and footy and going to the club dancing and arranging other social events such as picnics and going camping together. For some reason it was all or nothing. They needed the CYO name for the sporting competitions, I guess. I don't know. The air was thick with deep emotion. I felt sick and sad and tried to contain my feelings and control my disappointment and anger. I was anxious to extreme. I felt no one supported me or at least was not able to express that support on the day. They decided amongst themselves to close up, sell the furniture, and spend the earnings on a big end of CYO party to be held privately. Tables and chairs were sold off to the highest bidder. I'm not sure what happened to the snooker table or the pin ball machine nor the funds which were controlled by the treasurer and one other signatory. I bought four yellow plastic chairs and reserved them. Meanwhile it was back to the familiar back door to report to Fr Roche. He said the CYO was an agency of the Parish under Canon Law and he vetoed the decision to sell up. He said whatever funds were in the bank belonged to the parish funds and the furniture purchased by members from CYO funds were a donation to the Church of St Agnes' Matraville. He said to pass on his thanks for the donations but just as people donated windows and pews to the church the donors could not take them back and sell them off. I told him I could not control the sale, most of the stuff had been sold and taken home in members' cars already. I told him I had four chairs. He seemed close to tears and I could feel his frustration and loss of control. Nothing could be done. I had a final task, to get the keys to the parish hall returned, handed in via me to the PP. They agreed it was fair as they were not to use the hall after that day. So ended an era in the Catholic community in Sydney. The final active CYO had closed. I carried home those four yellow plastic chairs, two at a time, a hundred metres at a time. I held onto them as a fond memory of the good old CYO days of Matraville.

Also, during this period, I was invited to be a Catechist teaching SRE in local State Primary schools. I attended ten evenings of training once a year for three years. We had lessons in basic theology and in classroom techniques and use of resources produced by the CCD office in the city Catholic HQ, Polding House. I was interested in the lessons and learnt theology which the regular pew occupant got on Sundays at church. My education was far from a teaching diploma or degree nor any form or serious theology. Many of the kids were ok, some were restless and one or two were simply brats. However, if we were only visiting the school for 30 mins once a week and often had classes in storerooms and other students sat in the library reading, it is understandable that the 'Scripture Class' was going to be difficult. I never heard of perfect reports from fellow SRE teachers. At the same time, I was invited to be a participant in the pioneering service of an Acolyte. Ten or so years after the Second Vatican Council (Vatican II) held in Rome in the 1960s the Australian church opened up ministry at the altar to lay men over the age of 18. I undertook another ten-week program to train as an Acolyte. We felt so important learning about Sacred Liturgy, the Lectionary and other sacred traditions and spaces. I had been an altar boy from the age of 10 till 15, this was sort of a promotion. Girls and women were still restricted from the sacred space except to read the Word. Some people in the pews didn't understand we were lay men and thought we were training to be priests, though some of us were married men. Dad became an acolyte a few years later. Mum would wash and dry our Alb's with great care and pride. Unfortunately for many years she had to sit alone in the pews looking on. Cath and Anne and Pete had developed relationships and either attended church in other places or different times or not at all. I was soon to move on to another form of Ministry in the church.

Meanwhile, while still with Australia Post and doing the church stuff and with the CYO till it closed in 1979, I struggled socially.

I never had a girlfriend like most other young men, my peers. I did try but no one seemed interested. I had a few friends including some young women. Sometimes *I would* score a date, thinking it was of a romantic nature, but it was plutonic. No kissing or hand holding, no romantic evenings. Often, they were actual girlfriends of other men. Sometimes in group outings I'd ask other guys if I could dance with their girl, some said Ok. One girl though, Debbie, asked me out on a date! We worked together in the office and she asked another girl to ask me to ask her out. DB was keen on me. Wow! We dated a few times over eight months in 1979 -'80. It ended shortly after I asked, "have you ever thought of getting married?" to get her response "yes, but not to you." Seriously! We broke up. Mum was relieved because DB would sometimes sleep over in my spare room or on the couch but what would the neighbours think? Around that time, a 19-yr. old boy from the bush town of Wombat Creek, arrived in Sydney and stayed with his cousin who was a member of the old CYO. John joined up and soon asked if I had a spare room to rent. I did and he moved in with me. His dad was a cement truck driver and mum a nurse and he had a girlfriend Jan who lived in a town near his family. By that time, I had moved to be a team member of the regional youth organisation and was undertaking training in youth ministry leadership. The song, The Rose, was a theme of the training. We also learnt it's ok to hug others including men to men. John was quite silent and closed in and seemed like a rock at times. The songs Bridge Over Troubled Waters, and theme "I am a rock I am an island" were popular at the time too. I saw John as a rock. One evening he was walking by my room and I stepped out and hugged him. He began to quiver and cry saying he had never been hugged before even by his mum. We hugged often after that. John and I lived together for two years. Once or twice Jan visited for a weekend and she slept with him. I missed him dearly on those nights even though he was in the next room. I missed his tender evening embrace.

At church one weekend I saw an ad in The Catholic Weekly about PALMS, the Lay Missionary Service. They outlined several volunteer places in Papua New Guinea (PNG), and islands of the south west pacific. They offered an orientation program and asked for skilled people to volunteer on a stipend for two years. I wasn't sure so asked trusted people, the parish priest and dear Br Stephen Robinson SSG. The PP said to pray about it, but I was blinded by the adventure, Stephen Robinson said I should go. I applied to PALMS and got references from the priest and my office manager. The manager recommended I apply for Special Leave without pay for three years, he would approve it and I would be guaranteed a job when I returned.

    The week between Christmas and New Year's Eve, a mere four full days, was my PALMS Orientation program. The usual program would run three weeks but for some reason Barry, the PALMS coordinator could only manage that abbreviated time period. I took myself by bus and train to Turramurra station where I was met by Mary Gilchrist and so my association with PALMS and PNG began. As it happened, Sr Jane Frances and John Hickey her friend and Australian advisor were in Sydney and they met me for half an hour there on the course. Jane was the principal of the Catholic school at a small mission station called Malala on the north coast of Madang. Mrs Maureen Gleeson from Brisbane was also there. She and I were to go to Malala to work as teachers in the Secondary Education Centre rather than the High School as we were not fully trained teachers. While Jane arranged my work visa, I prepared to leave my home and family and my beloved Parish and the workplace. I was still living with John at the time though I never considered his opinion or feelings and emotions. He wished me well. Dad called to pick me up at 7am not wanting to be late for the afternoon "Air Niugini" flight to Port Moresby via Brisbane. Mum and the others stayed home, so I missed farewell hugs. John helped dad with my luggage, a huge brown hard suitcase bound shut with a leather strap. Two of my office mates were a welcome surprise farewell party, Marian and Marg who always had an ABBA hairstyle. They gave me an Aussie Swaggie doll and brought well wishes from others. I was wearing a Mission Cross with which I had been presented by the Parish who paid my fares up and back. My fresh passport was clutched in one hand and my shoulder bag slung across my body like a security blanket. DEPARTED AUSTRALIA was stamped and I was all alone heading off on my mission and great adventure.

Chapter 4
Papua New Guinea - Malala

Maureen boarded at Brisbane and was seated towards the rear of the QANTAS jumbo jet, John Hickey reassured us that he would be there and guide us through POM from International to Domestic and escort us all the way to Malala where he lived and worked. Maureen was much older than me, probably by 30 years. We knew little of each other but that we were to work at the same place somewhere in Madang Provence of PNG. The rest was pretty much a mystery and we put our faith in God and the church. Oh, and John Hickey.

Humidity enveloped the entire cabin of that aircraft immediately the front door was opened to the unbearable tropical heat of Port Moresby. My body was instantly covered in a warm sweat and I wondered if I could turn back rather than endure three years of this heat and humidity. I longed for the coastal sea breeze of Maroubra and the cool house with dear John and his happy face and perhaps a cold beer. For now, it was like literally being in a cloud. I stepped onto the hot metal stairs and down onto the melting tarmac and searched for the entrance to the arrival lounge. My long trousers and black shoes were definitely not the fashion for the tropics, but I wanted to look my best. Sweat seeped into my shirt and socks, streaming down my neck along the curves of my body into crevices I'd rather have kept dry. Gratefully the Australian department of Immigration had designed near waterproof passports! I did as I was told at orientation and queued on the Returning Residents line rather than with the hundreds of tourists and businesspeople. The officer examined my documents for volunteer visa and waved me through. I then grabbed my suitcase from the trolley and sort out the Quarantine section, which was actually, one man positioned behind an elevated podium looking down on us all as he surveyed the arrival hall. He asked if I had anything to declare and I said yes, I have a fruit cake. We were told to bring one just in case we were asked. He waived me to the exit. I asked if he wanted to see the cake. He just waved as if it were some sort of spy movie code word. "What do you have?" "Fruit cake." I was suddenly through and into the domestic side of the shed. I had arrived in PNG. Next to find John Hickey and Maureen Gleeson.

Maureen gravitated to me like a magnet as we found our next flight, *Port Moresby* (POM) to *Madang* (MAG). We checked in our cases and waited on the plastic dirty yellow seats feeling hot, confused and like fish in an aquarium. The terminal shed stank with dry sweat and we were surrounded by locals off the street searching for some airconditioned relief. Red beetle nut stains covered the fading grey walls which were decorated with old airline posters which had curled up corners and rips along the dry edges. Rubbish bins overflowed with drink containers and dead cigarette butts and unfinished food. Large fans failed to circulate the stench and humidity. John Hickey was nowhere to be seen. We stared at the two doors ahead of us looking for gate 6. Every time a plane took off or landed someone changed the gate numbers over the doors. One moment the left side was gate 3 and right was 5 then left was 4 and right was 2, then after ages the door on the right was labelled gate 6. Yes! We followed a throng towards a rust covered walkway which offered brief relief from the searing sun. We soon climbed the ladder onto the Air Niugini flight to Madang. At least we had cool aircon as we flew to Madang on the north coast via Goroka in the highlands. We were at last on our way. Again.

    Goroka was to be a quick stop over of up to half an hour, passengers off, others on and up again for the second leg to the coast. However, this was my first day in PNG and I was soon to learn what the marketing phrase meant to "expect the unexpected". After half an hour we didn't see any passengers approach the aircraft but there seemed to be some action by men in orange vests. We guessed usual refuelling or similar. Another half hour we were told if we wanted to stretch our legs in in the shade of the wings, we could alight but keep our boarding passes and passports with us and we could take hand luggage but smoking on the tarmac was strictly forbidden. A further ten to fifteen minutes we were told to make our way to the terminal building for a seat as the delay may take some time. So, we did, I caught up with Maureen and we sat together in the shed. This shed was like a tin barn with concrete floor, no ceiling, fibro walls and two large fans working against the humidity. Though it must be said that Goroka is much cooler than Port Moresby. After another while we were requested to go and collect our luggage which had been unloaded from the hold onto luggage trollies in the shade. I jumped up and got there first and asked a mechanic-looking man what the problem was to which he responded, "the plane is broken." So, we all went over and selected our stuff and some tried to carry it across the tarmac about 300 metres. I suggested we pull the trollies ourselves so some of the men pushed all the luggage to the shed. Maureen and I sat with all our two- or three-years' worth of baggage surrounding us. She clutched onto a black shopping bag or tote bag in which she kept her ticket, passport, a newspaper from Brisbane, set of glasses, spare specs, pen and paper, sewing requirements and other stuff if required. Maureen's black bag was to be by her side or in her grip every day and night for the next two years.

"Attention passengers for Air Niugini fight to Madang. Due to technical difficulties your flight has been cancelled today. However, we do have ten seats available on a charter flight departing soon. Those holding valid tickets..." before the announcement finished, I literally grabbed Maureen's ticket from her hand and stepped quickly to the desk, not standing back, I called out "two please!!". Eleven of us were escorted across to a twin-engine Cessna or similar. The pilot was busy unloading parcels and newspapers from any storage space he could find and loaded our luggage as best he could. One person sat in the co-pilots seat and was told not to touch anything. He didn't. The rest of us grabbed the first seats available. We all had window seats as there were five to a side. Luggage was shoved along the aisle and we held onto cabin bags on our laps. The captain called to the last one to slam the door shut. He did. Maureen's sticky tape would have come in handy to fix a slight gap in the left side near a window, but she had her eyes shut tight and rosary beads out slipping through her fingers at some pace. I don't think she looked up till we landed. I looked out my window to see women in the gardens on the mountains above the clouds. Someone pointed out the Ramu valley and we all gazed to the right tilting the aircraft about 20 degrees. Our captain asked us not to all look at once as we were flying through a narrow valley and we may hit the sides. We didn't. We just looked ahead for any sign of the Madang coast. We seemed to land across the runway straight up to the terminal shed. The captain opened the door and we all stumbled out. Soon Maureen and I were the last two of the eleven, even the pilot had gone home. In the corner of this shed was a public coin phone. I had an aussie 10 cents in my pocket and looked up: Catholic Church > Madang > Bishop. I dialled and Bishop Leo Arkfield answered. I told him our names and that we were just arrived from Australia for Malala. He hung up. Maureen asked what the bishop said. I told her 'Nothing', he just hung up. Next minute the attendant called: "*taim nau, yuplea go autsait*" pointing to his watch and waiving to the door. I got the message we had to leave. We stood outside in the blistering dry heat and dust. At least, I thought, we were in Madang, somewhere. I wandered over to the fence and peered through the cyclone wire to see a few men rolling cigarettes. They used tobacco and newspaper which was rolled by hand into a cigarette about 20cm in length. The smoke smelt sweet and most unusual. Maureen called asking what I was doing. I told her what I had seen and she exclaimed in a somewhat polite but exacerbated tone: "Paul, here we are sitting on the side of a dusty road, all alone in the heat, we can't speak the language, we don't know where we are, there is no access to a telephone, we don't have a car and the Bishop's call ceased without any hint of information, and you are telling me about strange men smoking cigarettes behind a tin shed." "Yes Maureen" I replied calmly as I gazed along the track beside the airstrip. The fence seemed to go on forever to the distance and opposite was a field of tall grass up to a metre in height. A small truck arrived, and the smokers climbed onto the back of the Toyota Hilux and it sped off to be enveloped in the dirty grey dust never to be seen again. Large birds circled above, possibly in search of food. We were tired and hungry too. Our throats dry and parched, beads of sweat streaming into those crevices once again. The sun was low in the western sky with about an hour of daylight remaining on our first day in this unexpecting place. I suggested Maureen stay with the luggage and I walk to Malala and get help. Maureen was never known to swear or curse, but I felt something like she did just then. She didn't need to say anything. I felt it. I stayed. Shortly, later when she had composed herself somewhat, she asked "do you know where Malala is or how far away it is?" A brief prayer passed through my mind, more like a desperate plea to be rescued.

    A cloud of dust appeared in the distance and from it soon appeared our rescue team. Sr Henrilena looked tired already after a big day of shopping and getting around town with Jane who despite dengue fever attended key education office and diocesan meetings in Madang. Jane had been with Bishop Leo when I rang and dashed out the door to come to us as he hung up with nothing more to say. It would have been good if he told me Jane was on the way, however here she was in a dusty car packed with groceries and office supplies and some hardware. With some rearranging Maureen was squeezed between vegetables and Henrilena on the back seat while I had stuff around my legs in the front next to Jane who had her white nun's habit hitched up due to fever. Every now and then she'd wind down her window and suck in air we thought hot but was refreshing for her. Our first stop was Madang town petrol station as the car needed fuel to get us to Malala and enough for a return trip as fuel was not available near Malala. Jane didn't have enough cash so spent her last Kina (PNG currency) on four ice-creams. Our first food in the country. Jane then drove the twenty minutes to a large Mission Station at Alexishafen which was home to two convents, a monastery of Priests and Brothers, a Lay Missionaries quarters, a primary school, church, various workshops including a garage, sawmill and an ice creamery, and staff quarters. Henrilena found food for us in her sisters' convent while Jane managed to get Louie out of his room and open the garage to fill her car. Louie was a German mechanic qualified in large factory machinery and heavy vehicles such as farm equipment, but he had to adapt to small cars. He trained local men in mechanics. He was a man of routine and showered after work before dinner at 6pm and listened to *Deutsche Welle* on his short-wave radio for two hours before sleep. We were soon on our way with full stomachs and a lighter load as some of the shopping was left with the sisters to be picked up in a day or two.

After what still seemed like an eternity we arrived late at night to our destination, Malala Catholic Mission. Maureen was given a room in the convent for the night and I got a room in the visitors lodging which consisted of four bedrooms and a shared washroom at the far end. Jane and Henrilena quickly swept the floor and made a bed for me as they weren't expecting us to arrive that day. I was quick to sleep despite the excitement and the sound of a swamp full of croaking frogs and a gecko in the room. That was my first day in Papua New Guinea. The real adventure was to begin the next morning in the shower.

Life at Malala.

Gerrard Doorakas called and knocked on my door at about 7 o'clock on Saturday 6th February 1982, introducing himself and inviting me down to breakfast to meet everyone. I said I had to shower first. There was only one tap in the shower cubical. The night before I had searched in the dark but didn't find a hot tap. At breakfast after introductions, I was asked about my first experience of life in PNG and I highlighted the one tap and realised that there was little need for hot water for washing in PNG but was assured I could get a hot shower in town, an hour and half to two-hour drive away, but not to bother as it's a dusty trip back! So, it was to be cold showers for my three years there!

I met many around the table that morning, most of whom had to dash off till lunch. Even Maureen had to go for some reason. Fr Jooren stayed behind a little for a smoke and he was off too. Others were the now familiar Sr Henrilena who was the cook and Maria her kitchen hand, Kate and Liz two Aussie women who stayed in the convent visitors' rooms, Joseph and Sheela an Indian couple, and as mentioned the school Chaplain Cornelius Jooren. Gerrard and his family lived in a house with a large veranda overlooking the community dining room. John Hickey arrived the next day. Lunch or the mid-day meal as we called it was served at 12:30pm. Coffee was available from the percolator all day and was refreshed at about 3:30 for after school cuppa time. Dinner or the evening meal was served at 6pm daily. A medicine bottle of Quinine was part of the table setting along with salt, pepper and tomato sauce. It was a bare wooden table with timber chairs, about six each side. We all had our favourite places, I preferred to look out across the dusty louvers to the garden and that large house. The opposite view was of the lounge section which had several old cane lounge chairs and a glass topped cane coffee table, and to one side was a television set and American 1inch VCR player. The concrete slab floor was covered with lino and on two sides were double doors. One opened onto that garden view, the other to a slight hill and facing the chapel. One other side of the recreation room was a blank dirty yellow wall and the other side was the kitchen accessed via a regular internal door behind where Fr Jooren sat at the head of the table. Once ever few weeks on a

Friday night we hosted others (i.e., Local or Native teachers) for a video movie which had to finish before *Lights Out* at 9:30pm otherwise the tape would be jammed till next morning and we'd all have to make our way home in the dark. Sun set at 6pm every evening and rose at 6am every day - give or take 5 minutes throughout the year.

There was a diesel generator for the campus giving power to all the teachers' houses, several dormitories, a full school of classrooms both High School and the Secondary Education Centre (SEC), the laundry, convent, our community room and kitchen, the visitors rooms the Chaplain's house the chapel which was as big as a parish church and the workshops which included a mini saw mill, the Infirmary or 'haus sik', oh and the Trade Store which was just outside the school fence. One of the senior and trusted boys of year 10 had the duty of caring for the generator he was older than others and may have had work experience before finishing school. Anyhow, the power was on between 6.00am till 12:30pm then from 5:30pm till 9:30pm. On rare occasions when Sr Jane or Clare Marie needed the electronic typewriter it would go later.

There were three recently constructed small cottages outside the fence on the road to Susure which didn't have power connected. I was to occupy one of them. They were near the market area and trade store then it was a stone's throw to the beach just across the road. I chose the house at the end of the line, closest to the beach so I could benefit from the sea breeze. Apart from no electricity, it was unfurnished and the southern side lacked an external wall above waist height so that everyone walking towards the store had an uninterrupted view of my washing room and there were no curtains on the windows which were on two sides, one facing the road and the other to the north on the side of the bedroom and the southern and northern ends of the main room. The rear or western side had no windows. So, there was the washroom with toilet and shower but no washing machine, and external door and the unfinished wall, a long front main room facing the road and two bedrooms, one without a window I used as my storeroom. There were no doors on the bedrooms. The front room had an external door to the north. This was sheltered by a castor oil weed which towered over the roof. The southern door was sheltered by a couple of pawpaw trees, a male and a female which bore fruit. To the rear was a coconut tree which occasionally dropped a dry nut onto the tin roof giving me a surprise and bit of a fright. The house had a ceiling and the walls had been lined too, except for the washroom walls, such as they were. The floor was a dusty concrete which had apparently dried too quickly and was rough like a footpath. I had to get power connected, the wall finished, curtains made, and some furniture. Otherwise, I was ready and eager to move in, and out of the visitors' shed. I was persistent and once I managed to obtain a key 'just to look inside sister', I held onto it. The sewing class made curtains of a floral material. I was issued with a bed and foam mattress, two sheets and some sort of blanket which was more like a thick rug and a large timber desk and a wooden chair. A student made a broom of coconut frond and I found a rag to clean the glass louvers and do some dusting. I managed to scrounge up a small table to hold a gas stove on which I could boil water for a cup of black tea or cook some rough dinner for myself on weekends if I felt so inclined. Some boys gathered together to make a wicker wall out of dried bamboo and they managed to nail it to the southern wall. At last, after several weeks, I had some privacy. My trusty kerosene lamp was my only source of light once Tommy had shut down the generator for the night. I soon learnt not to place the lamp on the floor when showering as the glass cracked! Silly me. I got a nail and hammered it into the shower wall and one into the toilet wall too. Sometime later Brother Kurt was visiting, and I asked if he could connect electricity to my house. He said he had no request from Jane, but he could do it next time he visited which I was told would be Tuesday after lunch. Five or six weeks later at the dinner table I asked Fr Jooren about Kurt, if he kept appointments. Kurt always said he would be somewhere on Tuesday after lunch, but not any Tuesday and it could be Friday or any other day of the week but Sunday, mostly. So, I waited and carried on with my kero lamp at home.

Meanwhile, I made the habit of sitting in a classroom of the SEC during study time between 7:30 and 9pm Monday to Thursday thus availing myself of electric light while preparing lessons and marking test papers or writing letters home. Sr Helene the SEC head teacher was happy someone was on duty too. Evening study time was pretty uneventful. One time though we endured an infestation or plague of grey moths. They were so thick in the air that several of us swallowed one of two. They came into the light and settled on desks, books and floors, coated all the library books, died on any surface available including fan blades. Study period was abandoned, and we all went home till the next morning when it was all hands-on deck with the brooms as by then the moths were several centimetres deep. Louvers were washed, desks washed, and floors swept several times. The whole library of resources and textbooks had to be rearranged shelf by shelf.

At the Secondary Centre five staff taught four classes – grades 7 to 10. Each class had about 30 students whose ages ranged between 12 and 22. Our students had for various reasons left school at grade-6 which was the first legal stage students could drop out of formal education. For various other reasons these students had decided to complete school education at later ages, some had worked in town, but most had lived a traditional life in the village. Most were from Madang Provence which was along the PNG north coast extending inland several kilometres beyond rivers and valleys into the foothills of the mountains. Some students came to the coast from mountain locations around Mt Hagen and Goroka and similar coffee growing areas which until about 50 years prior had not had contact with the western world. The highlanders were different from the coastal people in culture, language and physical build. They also struggled with malaria which was absent from higher and cooler altitudes. During school holidays it often took some days to get back home, usually on foot, and then to return refreshed with fresh food or a new shirt or a new pair of thongs on their feet.

    They were all enrolled in the College of External Studies based in Port Moresby. We were actually tutoring as the students were supposed to teach themselves in the village. There was no teachers' book or manual. Subjects taught were: Commerce, Neighbouring Countries, English, mathematics and science. I specialised in Commerce because Barry of PALMS, had said I worked in an office, so commerce was a good fit for me. I also taught Neighbouring

Countries to one class where we learnt about Australia, Singapore, Indonesia and some of the Pacific Islands. I also taught the study of Religion as I had been trained as a catechist back home. My understanding of the Bible and the Catechism was mostly limited to what I had heard from Sermons and Homilies by priests at Mass. I did my best. Barry was half right, I knew simple stuff about how an office works, simple taxation and wages, shopping and transport of goods and supply of services. However, I had no experience of book-keeping, Legers and Journals, reconciliation of accounts, Debits and Credits and all that stuff. I had failed commerce at school and was hopeless at Maths and I was asked to resign from a bank! The school had one calculator, other than that I just read one week ahead of the students and if they asked questions, we tried to work it out as best we could. Due to Maureen and I and others writing home to our parish communities and families some practical resources arrived by parcel. Exercise books, maths equipment and picture books of Australia - it all helped. The SEC had little funding and we relied on tuition fees and donations. The fees were cut to a minimum so that at least most parents could afford to pay from their extra income after market days or selling copra. Even those who had a job received the rural wage, which was much lower than an urban income, the logic being that rural workers had time to plant and grow their own food but town people had to actually purchase food at supermarkets.

Food for us volunteers and students were all planted and grown on site, apart from rice which was purchased weekly by the tonne. Every morning boys and girls went out into the sweet potato (kaukau) fields to harvest food for that day, then they'd peel it and it was cooked in a large kitchen for lunch and dinner. Once a day each student was served some beef which had been slaughtered earlier in the week by cowboys. Eggs were served by class group once a month, one each. Usually, tinned fish was mixed in with the rice and coconut juice soup which was always topped with *aibika* or a green leaf of some kind. Sometimes we had corn on the cob when there was a crop. In the staff dining room we were better off having meat every day but Fridays when we had tinned fish, usually mackerel in tomato sauce. We had eggs a few times a week but one egg each. Occasionally we had chicken rather than the beef and pork was off the menu as it was a delicacy saved only for major feasts such as Easter. One evening I was on duty at the students dining room and arrived to see 800 teenagers slapping tin plates and spoons on the metal tables as the food had not been served. They had yet to say Grace before meals due to the loud hailer having flat batteries. The poor girl on prayer duty tried calling out "in the Name..." but few heard. I called out over the din that the kitchen would be closed if there was not quiet. That worked! I never knew what I'd do with 800 meals of beef stew. Batteries were checked weekly after that.

In mid-1982 we had a change in volunteers: Sheela and Joseph returned home, meanwhile Pius Ep arrived from Switzerland to take control of the farm, especially the cattle. Pius was a very gentle and wise man, well trained and experienced in the care of cattle and farm maintenance. He and I became friends during his time at Malala. Gerrard and his family moved out to settle in Australia where his daughter was a natural citizen having been born in Melbourne. Sr Jane arranged for his house to be cleaned and painted so that the three aussie women could move there from their rooms in the convent or girls boarding house. Later she suggested that the community kitchen be closed on weekends and I *would* hang out with the women for meals at their place. We didn't like the arrangement being put on us including that the priest would eat with us too. He preferred to cook for himself on weekends and I arranged for a small gas stove and pots so I could cook for myself too though the girls said I was always welcome, and we often had Friday night drinks on their veranda in the evening sea breeze. We got to form a loose sort of community if not close friends. We were especially close during the bushfire season of 1982-83 when we were glued to our shortwave radios listening to extensive reports via Radio Australia. Kate was especially concerned as the fires raged around her home region of Gippsland and her hometown of Bairnsdale. We also listened to Maureen's weekly experiences travelling to town on Wednesdays for Sr Jane doing shopping and having lunch at the catholic HQ or Chancery office. She wasn't expecting that job nor did she particularly like it as she and all of us expected her to be teaching five days a week. As it was, she had her classes plus the Wednesday excursions. Mail from home was a major joy and connection to the outside world as there was no telephone and a twice a day radio Sked for Mission business rather than private communication. We had to drive into Madang post office and spend several dollars to phone home, probably once a month. John would write a few times a month. I'd receive several pages of hand-written news stuffed into envelopes to which I'd try to reply before the next edition arrived. St Agnes' Parish would send letters from parishioners and the Parish Priest would send a monthly supply of the Catholic Weekly newspaper and the parish Bulletins. Both mum and dad would write a few times a month and my brother Peter would dash off a page or so each time he visited home and read my latest mail. Cath and Anne also sent mail quite often, so I always had mail to read and respond to. I'd record the sender and date arrived and date replied on the back of each envelope and file them away to keep. Occasionally I'd get mail from my old workplace as well, but dear John was the most prolific and voluminous writer of all.

There weren't many connections with Australians around Madang though a few lived in the bush location of Bundi, two men named John and Gerard and a rather conservative priest by the name of Mike Morrison who was actually the local PP but who once said of Malala that whatever happened within the fence was up to them and he didn't interfere. Another was Barry Nobbs the PP of an isolated parish community, Bosmun, on the Ramu River. It was Christmas of 1982 that I visited Barry. On a Radio Sked I asked if I could visit there for a week or two, he agreed, and we met a few weeks later at the beginning of the school holidays.

Travelling to Bosmun was a journey relying heavily on the children I travelled with and their local knowledge. I needed all the assistance offered and then some. I learnt much about myself and the local culture and life in a small village and the life and challenges of pastoral ministry in remote communities. Remote from towns and the coast and communication and internally remote when considering people would literally walk for days to go to Sunday church once a month. Barry would travel in his small outboard tinny for hours then walk some to visit people for church ceremonies including administering the Sacraments of Baptism, Reconciliation (Confession) and Eucharist. Occasionally he had to sleep overnight in village churches. They invariably had a visitors' room attached where the priest would sleep in a hammock and the locals would feed him dinner and breakfast. I accompanied him a few times but not overnight. Travelling in his tinny was most interesting and often relaxing except for the day the motor kept cutting out due to dust in the air inlet on the fuel tank cap.

You may be wondering how I got to Bosmun from Malala and back. Here's the story:

At the end of school, a convoy of trucks and cars formed along the perimeter fence of the school and hundreds of students and staff sort out their transport back home or at least to Madang town. I had arranged to go with the Bosman students who found a truck heading toward Bogia. I jumped aboard with my small shoulder bag packed with two changes of clothes and toiletries and a small towel to soak up perspiration. The driver offered a seat in the cabin with him which I gratefully took. After several stops, we arrived at the regional town of Bogia where a change of transport was required. We were bound for the mighty Ramu and so were travelling to the farthest point west. Others headed inland to other locations on foot or by car if lucky. Our small company of half a dozen boys and girls jumped down off the last truck at the edge of the river and rested a while and someone arranged a canoe to pull across the river, some 100 metres or so. The river was at low tide and the riverbanks were deep and steep on each side. I was told I'd be first off, a privilege, I guess. However, I hesitated when confronted by a 20m high muddy bank towering above me. I asked where the track was. They told me there was no track, laughing at my expense. It was school holidays and we were all in this together. However, I had to go first. They said I had to make the track myself. "*yu yet workim road!*" I tried my best to clamber up the bank grabbing trees and finding a footing wherever I could. Two of the bigger boys grabbed my hand and guided me up to the top and then I was on my own. Single file was the way to go, keep up with the leader or be lost was the deal. Long grass and shorts and bare feet is not a good combination, at least I had my rubber thongs under foot. My shirt was soaking and my plastic cordial bottle almost dry of water. We heard stories of leeches and mosquitos, snakes and spiders, stinging nettle and got advice on which leaves to wipe our bum with should it be necessary. I carried some toilet paper but chose to hang on not wanting to 'pick flowers' with curious students looking on. There are certain things one didn't wish to share. The plain of long grass became thick bush or forest with cooling shady trees and a narrow well-worn soft track.

Barry had told me to look out for manicured lawns where I was welcome to pop in to see his neighbour priest. I was offered use of the toilet, a sandwich and top up of water. Refreshed, we set off again needing to reach Bosman by sunset at around 6pm. We had a few small but deep creeks to cross, some not too wide but one was particularly challenging. Imagine a deep frog and mosquito infested ravine with steep sides, muddy wet feet, thongs in hand for a better grip and having to cross on a moss-coated fallen tree log a bit wider than my feet. The look of fear and trepidation on my face must have been a give-away sign to my young and more experienced and nimble guides. Someone found a long stick for me. It was too narrow a bridge to hold hands for balance and the stick was useless and little comfort. I was on my own. They said "Teacher, if you fall in, we are unable to help. Good luck." I was determined, I had to go on. One foot after the other and I was soon on firm ground for another half an hour till we reached the Bosman River, a tributary of the mighty Ramu, with the church and village in view. One more canoe-pull and then a well-worn path up from a small wharf to go. Barry had a small shed on the riverbank where his tinny was moored.

    The young ones scattered off home and I strode up to the house next to the church, the only two western style timber buildings there.

Barry cheerfully welcomed me and after I had a chance to freshen up, we settled down for a cup of tea. This was to be my home for two weeks. Barry's home was a single storey construction of timber with a corrugated iron roof consisting of a length of five rooms fronted with a broad wooden veranda with steps in the middle as seen in the photo. There was one large main room which accommodated the kitchen and living room, next was the visitor's room with a simple single bed and a basic dowel rail to hang my clothes over and a hook on the back of the door for my towel. Next along was the narrow store-room-cum-office with a battery on a small desk and radio for the Sked then Barry's room, similar to mine but with a cupboard and table and chair. Finally, at the far end was the washroom with toilet and shower. Outside the washroom, in the garden, was the rainwater tank tower which was filled by operating a hand pump. The domestic water was directly pumped up the hill from the river and supplemented with rainwater off the iron roof. It was good advice to boil all drinking water but on a hot steamy day who could wait. Barry was a simple man though quite intelligent and knowledgeable. He kept in touch with world news and Australian current events via Radio Australia to which he listened daily each afternoon and evening. I accompanied him several times on his tinny, visiting local communities along his stretch of the Ramu, didn't see any crocodiles but was fascinated by river life and was treated to a symphony and light display of fireflies one evening. A couple of weeks with Barry was relaxing, entertaining and enriching. I learnt much from him and my stay there about life as a priest in remote areas of Papua New Guinea, PNG culture and the language.

    I learnt that village life revolved around the basic necessities of food, shelter and clothing, that family and community are the basic support or only support and services such as health care and church were add-on extras to daily life. Growing and processing food is a whole of community activity basically divided between women and men. The women and younger children did the hard work of planting and harvesting crops such as sweet potato, corn, herbs and other green vegetables called '*aibika*' and other food crops. Men helped clear the land of trees and rocks and built garden rest houses which gave shade in times of rest or '*malalo*' periods. Men and teenage boys constructed houses and community buildings from bush materials such as tall timber, bamboo and palm fronds or '*marota*'. The river and creeks were socially and environmentally sectioned for use as drinking and cooking water, laundry and kitchen washing and bathing and toileting. Women and men bathed in separate sections of the river while kitchen and laundry washing were in another section separating sewerage from drinking water. Each nuclear and extended family had their own homes while teen boys and young men often had separate sleeping quarters as did teen girls and young women. Older people and frail ones were cared for during the day buy family members. There were no clocks or watches, time was measured by the sun and moon. Breakfast had when it was ready after sunrise at about 6am, lunch later in the shade during a work break and all were home by the time the sun was low so cooking fires were lit, coconuts scraped, and meals cooked well before dark at about 6:30pm or so. Stories around the community fire happened after the evening meal and all were in bed well before 8pm or so. There was no electricity, light was by kerosene lamp, radio was powered by batteries, there was no TV in the 1980s, no telephone - land line or mobile, no road to the village and it was to be decades before the internet was even imagined. The ill had to walk or be carried hours to a medical centre where a person with basic nursing skills may have been in attendance. Basic medical care was given by a 'bare foot doctor' or Aide Post attendant. I had cause to visit the village aide post once when I suffered a fever, diarrhea and symptoms of malaria. He had no medication but recommended ripe bananas for the diarrhea, and water with sugar and salt for dehydration and aspirin for pain.

Heading back to Malala I was on my own without a guide or companion. Barry took me to the nearest road transport hub via his trusty dingy and car which he kept garaged on the other side of the river. It was literally the end of the road. Using my new-found language skills, I asked around for transport east along the north coast road towards Malala. No cars or trucks were going so far so it was a bit of a staged trip.

The first stage of about half an hour stopped under a large tree near a road side market and place where cars and trucks exchanged passengers and cargo and passengers could have a rest stop, buy some fresh food and find water and possibly a corner of bush for a toilet break. I was in desperate need of all the above, especially a toilet break. I was willing to forgo food for a quiet hole in the ground. Pit toilets are ok, but not my first choice. Luckily, I stopped outside a convent and grabbed the opportunity to introduce myself and take advantage of the catholic hospitality network. There was no time for chit chat at the door. I simply introduced myself as a missionary from Malala and asked to use the toilet as I was suffering *pekpek wara*. After that work of relief and a face wash, I was offered a light meal and a bottle of water for my journey. The sisters had some medication for diarrhea, a light brown tablet to take immediately and another later in the day. After half an hour of refreshment and sharing information and stories of Fr Barry and Bosmun and life with the other sisters at Malala, I was back at the market looking for the next car or truck heading east. This time I jumped aboard the back of a HiLux ute and found a spot surrounded by women with children, chickens and bags of food and a few men with their baskets under their arms or at their feet. Another half hour or so later the old man next to me woke from his slumber, saw me there and exclaimed *"O lo man! Yu kalap asde o tumora?"* which caused uproarious laughter and hilarity among the others. He had asked if I had jumped aboard yesterday or tomorrow! So funny. "*Asde yet*" I replied (Yesterday already). The laughter seemed to relax and cure me. I tried to sit quietly but everyone was curious as to why an Australian white man was sitting on the back of the ute and where I had come from and what I was doing there. I really got to practice my Pisin in real conversation compared to simply seeking information. This was one of my first immersion language experiences and set me up for what was to come.

    I was soon back in my little shack and had a welcome cold shower and rest before the evening meal. Everyone was full of Christmas stories and there was mail from Australia for me, heaps of cards and letters which I opened the next day as I was simply too tired. Among them a letter from dad that he had sent an air ticket so I could fly home for a family Christmas. Too late I thought but Maureen, Kate and Liz all said I should go, Sr Jane said go for a couple of weeks. So, I headed off to Madang town for an overnight stop at Catholic HQ and the next day I was home in Sydney.

      Dad met me at the airport with his big welcoming smiling face, took my bag and walked me to the carpark. Arriving home was a bit of a shock having been in the deep Ramu forests less than a week before. Now I was surrounded by family and people I hadn't seen for a year. It was good but surreal. Eventually someone asked about my hair cut, who did it. I said I tried to cut it myself with house scissors and a mirror in one hand. Oh! the next day I was taken to the nearest barber shop and mum told him to try to do his best. He did, cutting it as short as was decent in those days. A number 1 would have been best but that wasn't the fashion back then. He apologised and said if I could wait another week or two, he may be able to do something to repair my disastrous attempt. My hair looked like it had been attacked by a chook, pecking away randomly! I felt embarrassed but grateful that my family accepted me as I was. No one at church mentioned my hair but greeted me with open arms as I took my familiar place among them on the first Sunday back. The next day I planned to pop into the PALMS office in the city. PALMS being the lay missionary service or agency which sponsored me to PNG on behalf of my parish. The morning I was supposed to go, I called the office saying I felt cold and had to wear a cardigan but that I was still on my way by bus. I alighted from the bus in Liverpool Street before Elizabeth near Hyde Park. I just had to get out and felt ill. I walked into the nearest office which happened to be the State Police HQ and asked to use their toilet. They refused so I chucked up into their rubbish bin at reception. The Police gave me water and called my father who arrived in about 20 minutes and drove me to St Vincent's Hospital nearby. He took me to the rear entrance, probably the ambulance bay! I was asked at the entrance what the problem was. I told them I had Malaria. They said, 'we'll see'. You may not know but malaria is a reportable disease in Australia. Four days later in the ward the treating doctor and several other student doctors and nurses gathered around my bed. I was in a private room for some reason, probably that it is contagious, or I had to be quarantined. Anyhow, the doctor confirmed: "Mr Ward, you have malaria." I said, "yes I know, that's what I told them at the back door." I was free to go and two days later I was back on a flight to Port Moresby. Mum said that if they had known the effect of bringing me home, they wouldn't have done so. I wasn't to be back in Australia till the end of 1984.

    Life continued at Malala. Sr Jane found some work for me to do for the remaining weeks of the summer break. I was set up with textbooks and resources in a side room of the school office. I was to redesign the Commerce texts. I almost died doing that. Literally!

One morning the grounds man was using the grass slasher to cut the tall grass which had been let grow over the holidays. At that time, I was in that room when it a sharp stone was kicked up and pierced the insect screen wire and passing between open glass louvers finally striking and denting a metal cabinet immediately behind my seat. Two seconds before I had got up to grab some water, so the seat was vacant! Thank goodness! I checked and the dent was immediately behind where my head had been. I could have been hit between the eyes and killed or had one eye blinded and a rock in my head. Saved by thirst. I chucked the rock back to the garden and went to lunch appearing a bit shaken. So, I wasn't mauled by a vicious crocodile nor break my neck falling down a deep ravine in the deepest darkest forest on the way to visit Barry, nor was I surrounded and speared to death and consumed by savage head-hunting cannibals. No. I was missed by a speeding stone and lived to tell the tale.

When school returned, I was attached to the Commerce Department of the High School under the supervision of Sr Clair Maree. I taught each of the five year-7 classes in the high school plus some Secondary Centre duties. I still had weekly duties to supervise 6am garden work and in the first term break took care of the dozen or so lads who stayed behind to work or who were on punishment duty. I saw them begin work and gave them a meal of tinned fish and rice for lunch and similar for dinner which they cooked themselves. Teaching duties continued through term two as before.

    The weather moved from daily rain to the dry season and the water tanks were locked during the night to conserve water. There was to be no rain for six months as is usual for the equatorial climate. The ground dried up, dust covered everything outside and in. A grey dry film blanketed trees, rooves, vehicles which baked in the sun, grass turned brown and air-borne illnesses spread. Peoples' skin dried out and hair was dry and brittle. Skin diseases amongst the students and some of the staff were noticeable and the boys BO seemed worse than in the monsoon season. The lake dried and most of the frogs perished leaving a stink in the valley. On the other hand, the deadly mozzies died off too though some survived in puddles of stagnant water which hadn't evaporated in the relentless heat and dry. The overhead fans in the dining room brought some relief to the heat and a weekly scoop of Sr Henrilena ice-cream was most welcome and savoured to the last drop.

Tsunami!

For a while I had Thursday mornings to myself, not being due in class till period two so I took my time getting ready and enjoyed a quiet breakfast and strong coffee alone in the dining room. Then I'd freshen up and face the teaching day till lunch time. Liz, Fr Jooren and the others were in a particularly busy buzz when they arrived for lunch one particular day, even Maureen was chatting away in the mutual conversation. I must have had a look of bewilderment or something that caused them to ask "Paul, where are you going, what are you going to do?" I still didn't understand at all. Liz seemed to see I was in the dark on the topic of the day – "the Tidal Wave, what are you going to do?" This was the first I had heard of any Tidal Wave. "Weren't you at the special assembly at 9 o'clock? enquired Maureen. What special assembly? Everyone stopped and looked at me as I dug into my second helping of dry fish. Fr Jooren took over: There was a special announcement and information session this morning about the possible eruption of Kar Kar Island and Manum Volcanoes which may cause a huge wave. He explained. Maureen and Kate seemed to be in a panic. Pius, with some geographic background tried to explain about Tsunami but the others just called the phenomenon a Tidal Wave. Fr Jooren said that scientists from the Provincial office came to warn us of such an event and that even if we saw the tide retreat several hundred metres to expose the sea bed, we were not to rush in an grab any fish we could as the returning surge would cause more damage and reach inland possibly destroying school buildings in its wake. Someone said Tank Hill, being the highest point would be safest but given there are over 1000 people on campus plus local village people it would be crowded. Maria from the kitchen said she would run up the nearest coconut tree and live off fresh coconuts. I didn't know what I'd do but run up the hill. For a few days I carried my bible and a bottle of water and a banana in my bag, just in case. Soon the warning was withdrawn, and we all felt safe again and panic subsided. I'm not sure if I would have survived on 500ml of water and a banana for several days of sodden destruction but at least I'd have something to read. I wonder what the people of Manum and Kar Kar would have done. At least we all got some information about the relationship between volcanic activity and so-called Tidal Waves.

Chapter 5
Alexishafen, Papua New Guinea

It wasn't to be a tsunami which drove me out of Malala before my time. I had been invited by the Vicar General (the official representative of the bishop) of Madang to leave Malala and take up a fresh challenge. I was offered the opportunity of either Youth Work in the town which I declined or local community parish pastoral ministry which I accepted whole heartedly. I said my goodbyes to my friends at Malala and handed over my classes to others. As I'm never good at packing up I wasn't completely ready when John Hickey honked his horn and called me out to his car. I threw my suitcase and stuff into the boot of the white sedan and we headed off east to Madang HQ doing 60 in almost frigid airconditioned comfort. Two hours later I was dropped off and greeted by the bishop and his team and given an upstairs room for a week. Warm showers and town power were a most welcome change. The next week I was given my key to a room in the male wing of the Lay Missionary Quarters at the historic site of Alexishafen.

A mountain sojourn.

It would have only been a week that I was at Alexishafen when I was offered the opportunity of a couple of weeks on retreat to help me refocus on my life and new ministry. The retreat was at a cool location in the Highlands, specifically at Goroka town. Several people from across the nation participated in the days of reflection and prayer at Kefamo Conference Centre which was set in bushland a bit out of town to discourage excursions. However, one Saturday a few of us volunteered to dash in to get fresh supplies. Actually, I tagged along for the ride. I visited the book shop and newsagency but there was nothing much to do so I waited at the car for the others to return. The car happened to be parked in the shade by a wall opposite the pub where Aussies, Americans and other 'westerners' gathered for a drink. Soon a local man approached me and began trying to sell woven armlets for K1 each. He pointed to them saying one Kina, one Kina. A Kina is like a Dollar and is made up of 100 Toea. I wasn't interested in armlets and replied '*nogat* (no). He reduced the price saying '50 toea 50 toea', then tried 10toea 10 toea. I continued to show lack of interest in the armlets then his eyes lit up in a knowing sort of way. He pointed out a woman standing by the fence. A local woman in her late 20s I'd say. She was all dolled up in a most unusual fashion with stockings and shoes, a cheap purple nylon scarf and a western style dress fresh out of the Op Shop. To complete the picture, she was made up with lipstick and some kind of foundation on her cheeks. The woman had a fixed grin as if not to crack the makeup or disturb her pose by the wall. Let's say she stood out like a sore thumb, if you get the picture. The man continued: *Disla meri, em inap makim wanen samtin yu save likim. Em save givim gut long ol wait man. Meri ya em i cousin blong mi, olsem mi save gut long em. Mi save lukauim em. Olsem supos yu laikim, orait lo yu tude bai K10 tasol.* [this woman can satisfy your every desire. She works hard to please any white man. She is my cousin and I care for her. So, if you like it's K10 only today.] I declined saying that I'm a missionary. He quickly turned his back on the cousin and exclaimed "bloody missionary! - pointing to the armlets - ten toea, ten toea? I turned away and crossed the road and he moved on to the next foreigner. Soon my mates returned from shopping and we were back to safety at our retreat for another week of meditation. We then drove back down the mountain, through a settlement called '*wara-up*' - water up - or source of the river. That's the mighty Ramu. We continued through the cane fields in driving monsoon rain, six of us, three in the front and myself and two others in the back protected by a plastic tarp and the rain shadow. When the ute stopped, we got wet, when doing 60 against the rain we were dry enough. After a meal break, we were off again back to Madang and the north coast highway and I was dropped off at my new home. The next day I was to have my first meeting with my new supervisor.

Life at Alexishafen

My supervisor was Fr Anthony Patik SVD, the Parish Priest and Vicar General to Bishop Leo Arkfield, he and I had catch up meetings every now and then in his office just to see how I was going and to give me advice and encouragement. Once my weekly routine was clear, we had an arrangement that I'd use one of the parish vehicles and he the other. On his notice board I posted a note of my activities or appointments, so he knew when I'd have the grey car. Quite often I used an old bike as transport to locations of up to 30 minutes ride. The bike had belonged to a Bishop who used it in the 1940s. It was cleaned up with fresh tires and a new pump for me. It didn't have any gears, nor hand brakes but back peddling slowed it down and it came complete with a bell and reflectors. I had heard of a story of a Sister on a bike with no bell, but that is another story. It was a large parish extending along the north coast road and inland several kilometres.

    Sek was the common name used by most people for Alexishafen however it was actually the name of an island off the coast of Alexishafen, a short canoe ride away. I never journeyed to Sek Island though I wished to visit I never had the opportunity. The island people seemed so natural and peaceful. When I refer to Sek I mean the Catholic Mission station of Alexishafen. As mentioned earlier the compound included my home with four or five fellow 'lay' people including old Louie the mechanic, two Convents of women, a Monastery of men including Priests and Brothers, workers quarters including married or family homes which were in a row, and single men's dormitory. A major service provided by the Mission was a small regional hospital staffed by several sisters who were qualified nurses. The patients often arrived by car or PMV (Public Motor Vehicle) or walked in on foot. Families and friends had the responsibility to wash and feed the patients and often changed wounds. There was no Doctor at the Sek Hospital. The nurses observed, took readings and tests, diagnosed and prescribed medication and treated the patients. Seriously ill people were transferred to the Madang Hospital in town.

Three major activities associated with the Mission were the cattle project, the sawmill and timber plant and the mechanic shop. With the workshops, kitchens, a printery, the Post Office and warehouse, the primary school and garden maintenance crews, the laundry, a team of carpenters and a team of electricians, the Mission at Sek was a major employer in the Madang region.

Also, at Sek was an orchard of exotic fruit and garden of plants which was inside a fence for protection against thieves. Attached to the orchard was a huge store of freezers and fridges which was managed by a kind Brother who made all kinds of ice cream for us. In the middle of the compound settlement were a couple of lakes which were filled by springs from subterranean rivers. These lakes were surrounded by *kuni* grass a tall and thick variety of grass similar to reeds. The lake water was not the best and not used for drinking or cooking, also, Alexishafen was the last settlement along the road out of Madang which had town electricity.

Up the road from Sek but within the Parish, was the regional training centre for Catechists - people who worked throughout the Archdiocese of Madang at the grass roots level of proclaiming the Word of God and the official teaching of the Catholic Church as set out in the Catechism. The catechist's centre was a residential institution which housed several families per term. The trainees learnt education theory, language skills, and basic theology. A priest and his team operated that institution on behalf of the archdiocese. One of the team was a woman of German origin, Genevieve. She was often out on patrol to parishes around the area checking on the authenticity of the teaching.

Genevieve and her co-worker and compatriot Irmgard were the two women who lived in the Lay quarters. Louie the mechanic and I were the regular male residents. For six months or so a young English volunteer lived at the far end of the male residential block and of course the senior Australian by the name of Leo lived there as well. Leo did retire back to Sydney for a while but returned later till he achieved pension age of 65. Another older English man, Peter, lived among us for a while till he disappeared never to be seen again. From time-to-time visitors passing through would board with us for a few days or a week or so. We had two staff who tended the gardens and the kitchen and generally looked after the place. Between the dining room and men's quarters lived a family upon whose ground we lived. Genevieve and Irmgard occupied small cottages or what we would call studio apartments though we all shared meals in the dining room. Louie too had a separate room with on-suit. I had a room at the end of a long block or eight in the middle of which was the male bathroom. The bathroom was complete with a few basins for shaving and four shower cubicles all serviced by a choice of cold tank water or cold lake water or a mystery third tap. In the dry season it was lake water only which not only stank and left a green slime on the shower floor but also caused a long-lasting scalp irritation with damp flaky skin on my head. I guess I should have cut my hair short but persisted with my thick locks! Leo had installed a sort of solar water heating system consisting of a series of black painted pipes on the roof. That was the third tap! It was basically ineffectual.

    My weekly work was varied and at times exciting and very enriching and fulfilling. I didn't count the hours but did pace myself with two appointments a day and I made sure I had time to myself especially on weekends. At one stage however I did some Sunday work after Mass. As mentioned, I'd be off on my bike or driving the parish vehicle. My arrangements were made at the request or invitation of local church community leaders. I did write to all communities in the parish introducing myself so after a couple of weeks I had set up a routine. As the local people were mostly subsistence farmers, they planned their days by sun rise and sunset, and their festivals by moon phases. As I visited during daylight hours and each village had school children, our timing was around the school bus times. Morning bus time was around 8:30 while the return trip was just after 3pm. It was no use arriving before the bus in the morning as the people were busy with breakfast, washing and seeing the children off. In the afternoons, if I arrived just after the school bus it was best. Too early and the people would be away in the gardens or forest, too late and it was their time to cook for the evening.

    One particular morning I was on my bike riding to the base of a hill where I'd jump off and push it to the top where I had a weekly appointment with the locals. It was a beautiful location with a grand view of the valley down to the sea. This morning began the same as others, breakfast of juice and toast and strong coffee, then freshen up and begin my half-hour ride. Down the sealed road about ten minutes, then turn off onto a grass track, the kind made by vehicles with wheel tracks in the sand either side of short grass. This road led to a bridge which I had crossed several times before. I would always alight from the bike and walk it across as the planks were uneven. However, this day I tried to keep straight and ride across. I didn't make it! The front wheel caught by the V between planks and I was flung into the air landing on my back head down towards the deep valley below. I eventually opened my eyes and looked up to see the sky and my feet above me. I was desperately clinging to the thick grass lest I slide headfirst into the deep abyss below sustaining serious head injuries and broken bones and deep lacerations to my limbs on the way down, possibly not missed for several hours till dark at dinner time. Thankfully the school bus had not been by yet, I heard it approaching. As the bus approached, I thought I had a chance to be saved. If the bus driver or children didn't notice me, I would be there for hours as I said. I called out as loudly as I could "Kuni" the driver's name. Not sure if he heard me but he did stop the bus and came to help. He said, "*bike bilong yu bagarup na yu pundaun nogut long arere blong rot.*" - Your bike is wrecked, and you have fallen awkwardly by the side of the road. - how correct he was. He asked me to stand up, but I said I couldn't and was afraid I'd slip back into the deep valley. He offered his hand and again I was reluctant, but he insisted I trust him and grab one hand, then the other. He would assist me to stand and be safe. Trust! I had to. I was soon standing and shock myself off. I had cuts to both shins and grazed elbows, dust and vegetation on my shirt and shorts. My thongs were found in the long grass. Kuni picked up my bike and wheeled it to me before he jumped into the truck and drove off into the forest. I was still a bit shaken and dared not look back to where I had fallen. The front wheel was crooked so I straightened it as best I could and continued on foot to the top of the hill where I was greeted by the local village people. They gave me fresh water and a cup of black tea and something to eat, dry biscuits and a banana. Someone found bandages and washed my wounds and dressed them and I washed my face. I used this event to teach about how Jesus washed and cared for people. After a while I headed off back down to the bridge, walking my bike across this time! Soon I was back at Sek and lining up to be treated at the Aid Post / hospital where the nurse painted my wounds with ointment, or some sort of antiseptic locally called 'yot', I believe it was iodine. I then took my bike to Louie the mechanic who straightened the wheel and checked it over for me, wheeling it back to the dining room by lunch time. I was off again for my afternoon appointment after the post lunch siesta. I never tried to ride my bike across that bridge again. Thanks to the people of that village on the hill I didn't get another tropical infection.

For a year and a half, I lived and worked at the Catholic Mission, Alexishafen on the Madang north coast highway.

I saw and experienced much joy, happiness and laughter and contentment as well as pain, sorrow, injustices, and some illnesses too. I encountered people of deep faith in Jesus and God, faith and trust in the Catholic Church. Some with sheer devotion to the Sisters, Brothers and Priests among them. Few wanted us or myself out. Such was the power and influence of the Church in PNG in the early 1980s. Many village people also held closely their traditional spiritual beliefs in spirits of the earth and the natural environment, Animism. Some also believed in the influence of one or two powerful figures of their local community, those called in Pisin: "*sanguma*". A sanguma man tried to convince or control others in the village that he (usually a man), had a strong power over them and they had to provide him with favours such as gifts of money, pigs and other favours in order for them to prosper. If the garden or whatever didn't prosper, they were to blame and needed to respect him more and more. Some call this a Cargo Cult. Some people were so scared of the 'sanguma' they got ill and died.

Many other things happened in PNG, but these few accounts and stories are given to give a glimpse into my life there in the land of the unexpected.

My time in PNG came to a close in November 1984 after a period of close on three years of voluntary service to the community supported by both the local church and my home parish of Matraville and PALMS organisation based in Sydney. I packed a timber case, painted it yellow and sent it by cargo ship to myself. My bags were packed with stuff including some artefacts and souvenirs but it's the memories, some fond, some not so, that I carried back to Sydney with me. Dad greeted me with a huge smile as usual at the airport and drove me home for dinner. I was in a slight state of bewilderment and reverse culture shock for a while but soon settled back into life in Australia.

Chapter 6
Bathurst, Australia.

Following a brief return to my old desk in the Australia Post office in Martin Place, Sydney and a return to my family and the parish, I soon secured a pastoral job in the regional NSW city of Bathurst. Bathurst is about two hours' drive west of Sydney, across the Blue Mountains and down into the western slopes of the Great Dividing Range. The people of Bathurst claim it to be the oldest inland city of Australia. It is home to two major Cathedrals, Catholic and Anglican, a university campus and the regional HQ of the NSW mapping authority as well as a car racing track on Mount Panorama.

My home was in a flat at the back of the local Pathology service in the Coles carpark, next door to the outboard motor service workshop and opposite the town timber yard. Across the side lane stood the Bathurst electricity distribution point and across from that the NRMA - roadside assistance office. It was a short walk to the Post Office where I rented a PO box. Nearby was the Tucker Truck at the intersection of the Western Highway and the main road. It was in Bathurst that I purchased my first car, a Chrysler Ventura 3.5, 3 on the floor.

My work was with the Bathurst Catholic parishes mainly the city cathedral parish. I reported to the Parish Priest and was responsible to the parish council. The youth drop-in centre was an old-style schoolhouse on the edge of town opposite a park. The building contained a few large rooms and a small office which I made my own. The furniture had been donated by Vinnies and consisted of heavy old lounges and several chairs. A corner room had a TV set, another had a drink vending machine which I kept stocked. Communication with the young people was by word of mouth and a hand-written sign attached to the front door with sticky gum. I was on duty from lunch time till late, Tuesday to Sunday, with Monday's off. I couldn't get a regular volunteer to put the rubbish bin out on Monday night, so I did it myself. The youth had little to no ownership or sense of responsibility to the place or parish. Service was provided to them with little thanks.

Winter was bitterly cold in Bathurst, once or twice it snowed, otherwise it was frightfully hot and dry.

One of my fond memories was the night of the worldwide Live Aid concert for Africa which a few of us watched as we huddled around a gas heater. On my way home from work I saw a town irrigator which had frozen forming an arched ice curtain in the minus seven-degree morning. One night I was invited out for dinner and beers with two young men. One night in 52 weeks. Not even a cuppa tea with the parish priest.

My contract was not renewed by mutual agreement. I packed my car and drove home two days after the contract expired. Back to live with my parents once again. I began searching for my next job or phase of life.

Chapter 7
Melbourne. Pastoral studies.

Both my experiences in Papua New Guinea and Bathurst highlighted the need for formal education in the Pastoral arena if I were to continue undertaking pastoral work. Following enquiries and recommendations I applied to the National Pastoral Institute, Melbourne. Upon acceptance into the program, I bade my farewells to family and friends once again and flew south. Initially I was billeted with a family in the suburb of Aspendale on the Frankston line to the east of Port Phillip Bay. This became unliveable for various reasons so in due course I was moved to a room in a Christian Brothers' monastery in North Melbourne, just outside the CBD. The community there were all teaching in the school on the same campus. I felt most welcome and though not a Brother, I enjoyed their company at meals and in their community room. The NPI was located at Elsternwick and was attached to a Sisters' convent. Most of the students were Religious sisters or Brothers with a few 'lay' people such as myself. Almost all were sponsored by a school or institution, however I paid my own fees at NPI and my board and lodging with the brothers and all my other expenses for the year.

My plan was to gain paid employment as a Pastoral Minister or Associate in a Parish or Diocese the following year and to make a career in the field. I was happy to be a single man, not part of a religious community and not a Priest. That was my dream at least! The archdiocese of Melbourne under the leadership of Archbishop Frank Little, had initiated a program of Pastoral Associates who would be employed in Parish communities. I hoped Sydney would follow their lead and I'd return to my hometown in 1987.

The NPI was well staffed with qualified and experienced lecturers however the Diploma in Ministry was an in-church qualification only not recognised by secular institutions or universities.

My studies included: Christian scripture, Hebrew texts, Pastoral counselling, Moral Theology, Pastoral Theology, Adult education theory and techniques, and several specialist lectures including a set given by Dan Berrigan an American peace and social justice activist. Dan was a man of great personal inspiration.

I learned much about myself: my sensitivity to others and feelings and emotions; my need of and ability to express assertiveness; a basic understanding of morals compared with rules and laws; insights to scripture as being written in a human context rather than to be taken literally; an experience of Church beyond the male dominated parish; and a concept of sacrament and the Sacred.

Another man I met at the NPI who I came to know and love as a lifelong personal friend is Robert Nomonu of Bougainville, Papua New Guinea. Robbie was a young trainee Marist Brother at the time and had just spent a year or so in Fiji undertaking spiritual formation. In Melbourne he was studying Youth Ministry and we were participants in a few overlapping classes. Having lived in PNG just a few years earlier and as I could speak Tok Pisin, we held a common bond which continues to be strong between us. Robbie and I were to cross paths a few years later and again decades later under completely different circumstances.

It was in 1986 that I found a certain affection for Melbourne as a city with its own character different from that of Sydney. I was to return to this southern city later in life.

Following my graduation with a diploma in Ministry I returned to Sydney and my family home once again in search of work. The late 1980's was to be another set of adventures.

Chapter 8
Manager!

The Labor Government of Prime Minister Bob Hawke introduced the New Employment Entry Payment in 1987, under which I secured employment with the Christian Brothers institution as manager of their retreat centre at Mulgoa, western Sydney. The property of several hectares had originally been home to a family of pastoralists and included a stately stone mansion, a vast ballroom of solid sandstone, stables above which station hands had their quarters and several sheds and a 'shepherds' cottage' which stood alone in a field some distance from the main homestead. At the time of my stay at *Winbourne,* the grand homestead had long gone as a result of fire several decades earlier. The few Brothers and others on staff lived in the original stable building above the kitchen, dining room and spacious recreation room which featured a full-sized snooker table and a wonderful stone fireplace which was most popular during cool winter evenings. The Brothers had constructed a two-storey brick dormitory which housed guests who visited a few days at a time. The paddocks accommodated a small herd of cattle and old brother Vic had a pet donkey and several geese which he named Eeny, Meeny, and Miny. Had he had a fourth you can guess its name. I think Eni was his favourite. Another retired brother of the community was Efren, otherwise known as Eff. Team members, were Greg the director, young Vic, another Brother, and two Sisters Joan and another woman a New Zealander. The domestic team included a few cooks and cleaners and a maintenance man.

While this job brought some challenges, it remains one of my favourite occupations. The job description focussed on management skills and tasks such as directing staff, taking bookings, arranging maintenance and repair work as well as shopping and general management duties. With the agreement of the team, I also participated in some of the pastoral aspects of the program. I was mostly setting tables and washing up. Occasionally I'd escort a walking group along the Sydney Water Supply pipeline which ran by the property from Warragamba Dam.

Many happy times and moments of reflection marked my short time at *Winbourne*. I had to set time boundaries for myself as the others were Religious Sisters or Brothers who were dedicating their lives to the service of church and community. For me it was service for sure, however a paid job with time off which I negotiated to be Saturdays and Sundays as long as I was rested and ready to go on Monday mornings. Occasionally I'd stay at the shepherds' hut, taking my own food and trying to keep warm of a night by the fireplace.

One favourite exercise was visiting old Vic, sharing stories and a cuppa with him. Sometimes I'd help him with his geese at the pond. He had collected plastic milk bottles and tied them to each other along a length of rope which he stretched across the lake. His idea was to round up the birds by dragging the rope across the water to get them to one side. This method rarely worked if at all, but he made it a meditation. Another time, following a party, Joan and I secretly finished all the chocolates by carefully unwrapping each one and then forming the wrap foil as if full again. We had to confess later. No dessert that night for us. Part of the hospitality was to host school staff for a wine and cheese type of soirée on their first evening with us. The idea was to review the first day and plan the second or third days. Tradition held that the visitors would bring a good bottle of port while we supplied the crackers. However, one particular school had the reputation of being a bit stingy expecting us to provide everything. It fell to me as manager to find a port. The nearest pub or bottle shop was the Warragamba Hotel. I called and asked if they had port by the bottle and assured, they had I popped down the road after lunch to purchase same. I had never bought port before and was unfamiliar with pricing. Upon walking through the side door, I felt as if I was in a low budget western movie pub scene. All present, all men, stopped and turned to see this stranger in town who had dared interrupt their afternoon beers and game of snooker. They were all dressed in a similar style, that of a grazier or cattle man: old muddy blue jeans or kaki overalls, flannelette shirt, bushie's Akubra hat and big boots. Some sported full bushy beards otherwise they were unshaven. One big bloke bellowed out "You must be the bloke looking for port." "yes" I said, "How did you know?" They all laughed knowingly in a sort of deep tone. The publican opened the cellar which was accessed via a trap door in the floor behind the bar and soon emerged with a range of ports from which to choose. I selected the cheapest, not wanting to spend too much. Supper ensued as usual.

The conversation was polite and at times jovial. Some students were heard getting about after lights out so they were told to stand at the foot of the stairs for half an hour. After a while Joan saw them standing there in bare feet and exclaimed it was so cold on the concrete floor, they'd freeze their toes off. One laughed, the other smiled looking down at his feet which had a few toes missing already! Joan apologised and sent them up to bed. She felt so embarrassed. The next morning at breakfast Joan's story was the talk of the table. I got to tell of my adventure at the pub too when asked why I chose that brand of port. I said it was cheap. They all agreed but said next time not to go for Invalid Port as it was usually a favourite of poor drunks. Lessons learnt on the job by both of us. Joan is the person who called me 'manager'.

    Following scores of handwritten letters to Diocesan Bishops in Australia and Papua New Guinea I eventually received a favourable invitation from Gregory Singkai Bishop of Bougainville. He was interested in my offer to work in a volunteer pastoral capacity. He said that I would be working for the Diocese under the direction of Fr Herman Woeste, a Marist Priest of German origin. However, my time at Mulgoa was extended while I awaited notification of my Visa approval from the Papua New Guinea consulate in Sydney. Soon I was assured my visa would soon be approved so I returned home to pack and bid my farewells to family and friends.

I was to spend many an afternoon enjoying the hospitality at the consulate. Following several international calls direct to Andrew of the department of foreign affairs and immigration in Port Moresby, the Sydney office eventually issued my visa and I was off to PNG the next week!

Chapter 9
Bougainville, P.N.G.

I was to work in the *'RENBO SEVIS'* Rainbow Service based at the Rainbow Centre, Koromira.

My journey took the usual route from Sydney to Port Moresby via Brisbane. From POM is was north east across the eastern mainland to the small airstrip at Aropa, just south of Kieta, the former colonial capital of North Solomon Provence. I was met by a young local priest and driven to the catholic HQ nearby where I spent a few days orientation in the bishop's house along with a few others on the diocesan staff.

Gregory Singkai was a native of Koromira village and the first indigenous man ordained Bishop of Bougainville. When asked once what I thought of him, I said he was a proud man. He questioned what I meant by 'proud' indicating he thought it to be negative. I assured him it was meant in the best possible way, that he was proud of his birthplace, his people and his island of Bougainville. The bishop seemed to be happier with that explanation. I had noticed the posters and leaflets around the church proclaiming '*Yumi yet i sios.* We ourselves are the church'.

Indeed, Bougainville people and culture are somewhat different from that of the mainlanders, whom they nicknamed 'redskins' due to the red tinge to their brown skin tone. The Bougainvillians having a pure black skin. They belong to the ethnic and cultural group of the Solomon Islands. Bougainville island is several hundred kilometres in length with a mountain range forming the physical spine of the island and a fringe of glorious black sandy beaches, swaying coconut trees, and a main road on the eastern shore which passes through major centres including Arawa, Kieta and Aropa and down via Koromira to Buin, crossing creeks and fast flowing rivers which pour down the mountainside to the Pacific Ocean.

The island people of Bougainville stand tall in their presentation of confidence, willingness to act and strive for truth and justice and democracy. At the RENBO centre lived the Priest, his house keeper and a group of young men who were participants in the rehabilitation program. Physically, the young men, are strong muscular and handsome looking in appearance. They lived in a shed by night however their daily activity was in the physical construction of several timber buildings which became the Rainbow Centre HQ and hall and education rooms.

You can imagine how physically fit these young men were. If only I were not restrained by my position in the Church and social and religious expectations placed on me and my behaviour! I felt trapped as a gay man in a foreign culture, in a difficult social situation. Internal conflict troubled me and at times boiled over into my behaviour. On my desk I had a small photo of a former 'girlfriend', the Australian woman I had met in Melbourne and who had gone to Tonga. She had led me on but dropped me for another man. However firstly; it wouldn't have worked out but secondly; I kept her image as a form of lock to the door of my gay closet.

My supervisors apparently noticed my predicament and reported to the Bishop who contacted PALMS back in Australia. I was moved to the Bishop's house for a while. After a week or so the PALMS coordinator called me himself and broke the news that I was to return to Sydney as soon as I was ready. My time on Bougainville came to an early close.

I had had the privilege of spending Christmas 1987 in my friend's village and experienced other highlights such as; a near drowning on Koromira beach, visiting the mine pit at Panguna, being berated and educated by local counsellors in the sorry history of 'Black Birding' - slave / indentured workers on Queensland sugar cane farm, and learning the art of negotiation in a community reconciliation context.

Chapter 10
Getting settled again – 1989 -'92

"Time to get out of bed Paul!" came the wakeup call from the kitchen as I lay there well after sunrise. The six months or so following my return from Bougainville felt to me as if I was in a deep fog, uninspired to do much at all. Looking back, I was in a state of shock and depression. Anxiety was too much of an effort at that time. Mum and Dad were loving but tough. I'm not sure what they made of my mental and social state. I had to look for work, play the game to the rules of the Department of Social Security and the Commonwealth Employment Office. Ask employers for jobs I could never do in order to complete the spaces on the bottom of the job seeker form, have it stamped at the employment office, walk two blocks to the DSS, line up to be spoken down to by a clerk behind an iron grilled window, then have them stamp my application for government benefits and take the bus home again till the following fortnight. A cheque would be attached to the next fortnight's form which I'd deposit into my Commonwealth Savings Bank account, then line up again at the withdrawals counter to access my savings five dollars at a time.

On Sundays, I'd drag myself to church in fulfilment of my catholic duty bound by Canon Law in fear of eternal punishment if I failed to practice my religion according to the rites of the Holy Roman Catholic Church. After some months I felt comfortable again, comfortable in the church, playing the role of Acolyte dressed in my white Alb which mum washed and hung out to dry on the back clothesline. I once again felt needed and wanted in the church.

Eventually I found a job with the State public service in the Local Court building The Downing Centre, in the city. The building had been home to a woman's fashion house (It had been a department store, known as Mark Foy's) and to this day is painted a ghastly off-orange, sort of mustard colour and the exterior promoting garments such as gloves, hosiery and corsets. Filing court papers and sorting printouts was so easy. So remote from the jungles of Papua New Guinea. I found a life of regular hours, regular bus times, regular meals and routine beyond one's wildest dreams. Just what I needed to settle me once again. The job was always temporary, two weeks at a time. Each Friday fortnight the manager would call to me as I clocked off 'see you on Monday'. I had work for another ten days. While it was interesting and steady work, I was on the lookout for church work, this time in Australia.

I had to take one day off to attend a job interview for the position of assistant house master at a boarding school in Bowral, south of Sydney. It was in youth ministry for which I was somewhat qualified. At first, I wasn't offered the job and I continued filing court papers for another four or five weeks as I sent out applications for other positions. One evening at home I received a long-distance call from Fr Bolt the school principal inquiring if I was still available as a position had opened. I said yes and he invited me to pack my bags and travel down to the school as soon as I was available. I gave a week's notice and off I went.

Chevalier College Bowral was to be my next home and workplace for eighteen months. Upon arrival I was called into the principal's office. I was expecting Fr Tony (Father Anthony Caruana) to be there as it was, he who interviewed me earlier in his capacity as senior Boarding House Master. To my surprise Fr Bolt told me Tony had been suddenly re assigned and sent off to the Missions in India. I was to take his place at his boarding house, meanwhile a married man had been promoted to Tony's position and he would be my supervisor. I was happy to have a 'lay' man supervise me rather than a priest or brother. That night I took my place in Tony's old quarters consisting of a bedroom, office and bathroom. One door opened onto the courtyard which led up to the Monastery where I had meals and afternoon tea, the other door opened directly onto the boarders' dormitory. From my vantage point I could see most of the boys, those in years 7, 8, 9 and 10. The year 11's had a large room to share and the year 12 boys were housed in the attic above my rooms. As I made my bed that first day, I turned over the old mattress to discover the latest Playboy magazine. I promptly destroyed it and told no one of it at the time.

    The Monastery was a grand timber construction housing the priest and brothers who worked on the school campus. One retired brother helped in the school canteen and laundry as well as following his passion writing letters on behalf of himself and Amnesty International to leaders of governments around the world and other national and international Non-Government Organisations. This humble man was also the brother of a powerful Australian Archbishop. Other occupants included the Principal, the head teacher of Religious Education, and until recently, the head of Boarding, among others. While some of the Religious community and myself lived in separate quarters, the monastery was the focal point of the community who lived there. We all assembled for breakfast at 7:30, lunch at 12:30 and dinner at 6pm. I was very much a visitor, though privileged to dine and share time with the others on their veranda. I was in no way interested in or attracted to their monastic way of life, though the meals were hearty and filling and the company warm and welcoming. I must point out here that my salary package included a stipend or monetary allowance, meals and accommodation and occasional use of a vehicle for work duties. It was a very comfortable setting. The work and social life however were another story!

Apart from the welcome at the monastic community and chatting with some of the others on staff such as the laundry lady and the visiting nurse, I had no real friends in town. I had left any friends and family back in Sydney. Going home to my family was a bit of a stretch however I did find time on my Mondays off to take the train into Sydney city and have lunch while spending a few dollars on the poker machines at the City of Sydney RSL. Another club I frequented of a Sunday night was the local RSL. I'd usually stay in local motels in a neighbouring town on my night off. No one came down to visit me and I rarely visited home or others. I was comfortable but without close social contact, though I did enjoy the company of that retired brother.

Although I was originally interviewed and employed as an assistant house master, with a change in administration over the summer holidays, I was offered a change of occupation, that of Canteen Manager plus other duties.

One of the 'other duties' was that of infirmary attendant. To this end I was moved from rooms in the boarding house to a room in the infirmary. If students had to sleep over in the small infirmary and may need assistance of a night, I was on call for them. This involved making sure they took medication, had a meal and fluids and so on. Nothing medical, just supervision. It was rare any boy would call at my door during the night.

Another duty was the cleaning and polishing of the assembly hall parquetry floor. It had to have grip for indoor sports such as basketball but had to have slide for dancing. This part of my job ensured I had plenty of exercise and built-up muscles in my arms from mopping and using the polishing machine and in my legs from pulling that machine around too. Yet another responsibility of mine was to hold the keys to most of the buildings around the campus including the squash courts, the chapel, boarding houses, laundry and of course the canteen.

Running the canteen took about half to two thirds of my weekly hours and involved arranging the volunteers' roster of people to serve in the canteen, banking, purchasing stock and serving the hoards at school meal breaks and opening the shop twice a weekend for the boarders. During meal breaks I had to think quickly calculating the price of goods, accepting cash and giving the correct change. There was no time to use a calculator and, in those days, there was no such thing as eftpos. A challenge came when teachers approached me asking not to sell fizzy drinks or heaps of sweets especially those with red colouring because some students turned up at class after lunch on a sugar high! Try telling teenagers there is to be no more fizzy drink available during lunch! Then came the challenge of 'healthy donuts! consider that concept for a moment. I took the challenge to the local town baker. He created a recipe for wholemeal donuts which were light in texture but with way less sugar than regular donuts. He tried to offer then at a reasonable price so I could sell them with some slight profit. This item was not, I have to say, a high demand product.

    School holiday duties were where I really shone, my hospitality skills came to the fore! As the boarders were away and I was still on campus the school manager got me to be hospitality liaison person when we had visiting groups. I was told how many visitors to expect, any special requests or requirements and so on. I had to liaise with kitchen staff and others regarding mealtimes and any dietary requirements. Other duties included guiding the visitors around town and the campus, making sure facilities were clean and open for them and locking up after use. Almost all the groups were so pleasant to deal with. They included the

Christian Cricket Association and the NSW Country Cricket groups. One group was booked by the former principal before he left office. He had offered a flat rate and very basic quote not taking account of their special requirements and ongoing updated requests. They supplied their own Registered Nurse who dispensed medication to the participants. Team members slept in the infirmary and one parked his Harley Davidson next to his bed! I managed to get him to park it undercover on the veranda where he could see it. They insisted on any religious images be covered or removed as they were a totally secular and some of them claimed to require kosher meals depending on their hunger and the smell of the food. Our new principal consulted me and others on staff before taking a booking for that group again. It was unanimous, they were too demanding, and the school made a great financial loss, so they never visited again. However, I did learn how to hide a grand piano in full sight!

Moving towards the inner Catholic circles

Towards the end of 1991 I began enquiries with the archdiocese of Sydney regarding a vocation, a calling to the Priesthood. Michael Foster was my contact person being the director of vocations. However, Michael challenged me asking for a case to be made for me to apply for Sydney rather than Parramatta,

Wollongong, Bathurst or Melbourne as I had lived in each of those dioceses as well as Sydney. I convinced him that Sydney was best suited for me as it was my natural home, my birthplace. He then challenged me on his concern about my education and my ability to complete tertiary studies. In order to test the vocation and my academic ability I returned to my family home and enrolled in the University Preparation Program with the University of New South Wales. There I studied foundations in academic education and Aboriginal Australia. I'm happy to say I passed with distinction at the end of the academic year.

Catholic Mission talks

Meanwhile, I needed money to live and pay my share at home. I also wanted to foster church connections prior to my academic studies in theology and formation as a student for Ordained Ministry (Priesthood). To that end I contacted PALMS the lay missionary people who put me in touch with the Catholic Missions Office located at Ashfield, Sydney. The CMO offered a small stipend or allowance and arranged accommodation and meals in exchange for public speaking at churches for a weekend. Put another way: I would be assigned a parish to visit and the name of the parish priest and the location. I would prepare a five to seven-minute talk on my experience as a missionary and the priest would provide a bed and meals – usually Saturday evening dinner and Sunday breakfast. I would speak during each Eucharist of the weekend except Sunday night. The aim was to both inform parishioners of the work of catholic missions and to raise funds for the organisation. On the first objective I succeeded but on the second I managed to raise less money in donations than others. I didn't really like the idea of fundraising and directly asking for cash or credit card donations.

    I did learn a few things about the life of priests and living in a priests' house. Most were very hospitable. However, others! One priest directed me to the local Community Club for dinner which I had to buy myself. He arrived at reception, not being a member as others are, he simply asked reception to page any member of the parish to come to sign him in, he then expected that person or family to naturally invite him to join them at their private table and pay for his meal and drinks. So, the receptionist announced: "attention members and guests, Father Joe from Saint Happiness Church is at reception. Would any member of his parish please come to reception to sign him in?" He had it made. Another pointed me to the deep freezer where if I were able to dislodge a frozen plastic bag of unknown substance, I was free to have it should it defrost in the microwave within an hour. Another man grew his own vegetables and was a strict vegetarian and spartan eater. He expected his visitor to survive on one cup of home-made pumpkin soup and a slice of dry bread. A banana was offered for breakfast and as much filtered water I could drink. Then there was the priest who sat me down upon arrival and read my notes. He offered a sure-fire way to raise heaps of money. I listened carefully. He said to tell a story of how, on one hot sweaty day in deepest darkest Africa I was travelling along a remote jungle track avoiding wild tigers and listening out for elephants crashing through the bush while with an eye out for snakes and poisonous spiders when I heard a poor little black girl crying as she lay on the ground under a coconut tree. Her clothes were torn and dirty, her hair needed washing and she had been attacked by an unknown person or beast, and left with bruises, cuts and a broken hand. I picked her up and carried her miles to the nearest missionary house and gave her medical attention. The priest said people like such stories. I said I had never been to Africa let alone met a girl in such a condition. He told me I could adapt saying I was in Papua New Guinea where wild pigs roamed and so on. I thanked him for his advice. That night at the Saturday vigil Mass I took my turn to speak. I walked up to the Ambo from where I was to 'preach'. (the Ambo, otherwise known as a Pulpit) I greeted the people and thanked the priest for his hospitality. I began: "Dear people, I could tell you a story about how I was in the jungle and came across a poor young black girl covered in sores and how I carried her to the safety of the local Mission. However, I will tell you what actually happens." I didn't receive a favourable report from that parish and wasn't invited back. Not sure why! Such was my humble introduction to public speaking and a basic form of adult education.

Introduction to Hospitality
This source of income with the Church dried up and as it wasn't considered formal employment, I soon became eligible for a Labor Government subsidised six-week Hospitality course at Paddington TAFE. This I lapped up! We students were supplied with a full 'black and whites' waiters' uniform including leather nonslip shoes, black socks, two white shirts and black trousers and a waiter's knife / corkscrew. I found my natural abilities and upon reflection, should have pursued a vocation in hospitality, it suited me well. I was to have further opportunities in this field later in life. Why didn't I listen to the spirit? Anyhow, I learnt the fine art of greeting customers, carrying plates and glasses, and well, I can't say I learnt the art of 'silver service' one example says why!

As part of my practical learning, I was assigned to work at an international event at Darling Harbour Convention Centre. There were hundreds of participants to serve, eight at a table, and I had three tables. It was a top-level event. Silver service as the standard expected. I had done three hours in TAFE trying to carry dry beans between a spoon and fork and serving stale bread rolls on a spoon! Seriously! Back to the event. Tables were set with cutlery, glassware and crockery. Food wasn't carried to tables on plates. Oh No! We were given layers of starched white waiters' cloths with which to line our left arms in protection from the solid silver platters of vegetables and meat which were received directly out of the 80°C ovens. Tongs were forbidden, sparkling silver serving spoons and large forks were to be used. Serving the dinner rolls went off well, I didn't drop any on the floor and into a client's lap. Then came the roast meats in gravy and baked potatoes and those pesky peas. I was sweating like a pig on a hot day in the deepest jungles of Africa! Perspiration may be expected on the brow of a waiter fresh out of the kitchen as he or she carried hot platters on his or her arm several hundred metres across an enormous dining room in a cavernous exhibition hall. However, this waiter had sweat streaming down his face, off his nose, rolling across his lips and falling as if a tropical storm onto the plates, bald heads and laps of guests who had forked out hundreds of dollars for the privilege. Three other waiters were assigned my tables and I was sent home after serving (that term used loosely) one table! Silver Service was not, is not, and never shall be, my favourite form of delivering meals! I wasn't invited back.

Better fortunes awaited me in the very civil and cultured environment of the NSW State Parliament House on Macquarie Street, Sydney. After three shifts in the Strangers' Dining Room, I was invited back for paid employment several days a week, as many hours as I was available. Fifteen dollars an hour was top rate pay in those days and double shifts were on offer. Hard labour at times, pulling tables across carpet, setting for 250 to 300 places, serving several tables, clearing and resetting for the next shift. Then there was the polishing of thousands upon thousands of individual pieces of silver cutlery from butter knives to dessert spoons and everything in-between. I loved the systematic work. Very methodical, organised and somewhat regimented. What a location too, sweeping views of the Domain from behind the parliament house and Sydney hospital back to the Opera House. Did you know the Speaker has their own suite of rooms including lounge, large timbered office, private dining room and bedroom with full bathroom? I had a sneak peek one afternoon as I cleared the Speaker's dining room following a late-night party, a soiree indeed, the night before. Actual Champagne, top shelf liquor, fine wines and platters of fruit, caviar and fine cheeses had been served.

This period, though brief, was one of real practical learning. Teamwork, working with colleagues, time management and undertaking a range of hospitality tasks from: setting tables, washing up, plating food, table service and pouring wine at the table among other tasks, were all of great benefit to me personally and in my future employment.

Epiphany House

Following on from my enquiries regarding the Priesthood with Fr Michael Foster, the process developed week by week, month by month till Michael invited me to be a foundation member of Epiphany House located in suburban Sydney.

Epiphany house was quite a strange place to live in several ways. The actual building, the location and the people there, especially some eminent visitors. The building had originally been dedicated and blessed some decades earlier and had recently been vacated by a community of Sisters. The woman had all retired and the community had decided to move to more appropriate accommodation for women their age. The Catholic Archdiocese of Sydney purchased the two-storey residence for the purposes which were somewhat unclear. It was up to us the first occupants to form a community identity which would develop and modify over the coming months and years. Such an exciting moment in the lives of we the originals.

For me, this was to be a year of discernment prior to entering the formal Seminary period of formation and education. Several men moved into Epiphany House including a bus driver, a courier driver, an immigrant from Tonga and a man who played piano, oh and Michael, the chaplain and Director of Vocations.

I was there from day one when we were given an archdiocesan cheque to go shopping for whatever we thought was needed to feed six men for a fortnight and to set up a domestic home. I held the cheque! What a shopping spree we had! We raided a warehouse and filled several trollies and carts with everything from an iron and ironing board to fresh fruit and vegetables to light globes and electrical extension leads and two ten litre containers of ice-cream, vanilla and chocolate. We put all the goods through the checkout and were asked to pay, so I produced the cheque and filled it out to the amount due, some several hundred dollars. It was a hot Saturday afternoon and we were eager to get back and unpack and load up the fridge and freezer. I presented the cheque drawn on the operating account of the Catholic Archdiocese of Sydney but the manager refused to accept it. We pushed the load to the entrance of the warehouse but the manager still refused to accept it. I said it's from the Catholic Church and that institution has heaps of funds to cover the cheque. He agreed but said he didn't have that particular organisation on his list of approved accounts. I looked at the frozen goods and pointed out the ice-cream. I said that until we paid for the goods they belonged to his shop, he agreed. I said his ice-cream and frozen peas were melting in the blazing summer heat. He soon took the cheque with the name and address of Michael Foster. We loaded up the courier van and headed home with the food and cleaning products. Ah the power of the church and money, and melting ice-cream. Every such church institutional residence has to have a blessing and opening and a commemorative tree. I not only had a chance to work on the hole for the tree, I also was given the responsibility of accompanying his Eminence, Cardinal Clancy, the Archbishop of Sydney as he blessed the building and garden with holy water. The man didn't even know which page in the ritual book he was up to during the ceremony. I've discovered that bishops actually don't know much due to their total reliance on others to assist and guide them at every turn. As I've mentioned earlier, I used to work with Ken Clancy, the archbishop's little brother, at Chevalier College. Ken was aware of what was going on around him. The two siblings were quite the opposite in their understanding and practice of the Paradigm of Service in the catholic community. Ken lived in a small bedroom and shared a bathroom with others in a humble monastery and wrote letters seeking clemency for political prisoners, while his big brother lived in the Archbishop's Palace in the grounds of the Sydney Cathedral in the city and worked in an office building occupying a whole floor which was accessed only by security coded doors. Not getting into a deep discussion of the theology of church at this point, let's move on.

The group of men who occupied the residence were far from a 'community'. We all had our 'day jobs' and came and went as we pleased except for agreed shared prayer time in the evenings and weekly Saturday morning Eucharist. We shared household duties such as cleaning, shopping and cooking. I certainly never saw or related to the others as 'brothers on a journey' or similar.

Easter that year was to be one of major significance in my life, not that I knew it at the time. It wasn't anything particularly catholic or religious or spiritual but a chocolate egg. Not the actual egg, but what happened in the dining room on Easter morning. The evening before we all attended the Cathedral celebrating the solemn rites of Easter, the 'paschal mysteries. Sunday morning was more of a relaxed atmosphere. We shared breakfast and later shared Easter cards and Michael gave us each a chocolate egg. Mine was a big as a football, round and hollow. Very traditional. All my life I had opened the eggs by gently peeling off the alfoil and squeezing a section to break into the egg. This year I wanted to crack the egg by bashing it on the table. I tried once, tried twice but the egg failed to crack. The third time I lifted it higher and bashed it heavily on the table causing a noise. The others jumped back in some sort of fear or fright. One guy, the courier driver, thought I was angry or had lost my cool and apparently confidentially reported what he thought to Michael who duly recorded the 'egg incident' on my file. I don't recall Michael mentioning the 'incident' to me asking my version of events, he was however a witness as he had given me the egg. This was a case of actions speaking louder than words. Easter eggs are symbolic of new life however the breaking of my Easter egg that year became an incident to be recorded with interpreted symbolism.

My studies in a Bachelor of Theology had occupied my mind all year. I commuted between home and Manly by train, ferry and bus, a 2 / 2½ hour round trip. Some days I had morning lectures beginning at 8:30am so had to leave home by 6:30 or earlier with the commuters and some days finished at 7:30pm after dinner. I paid my own tuition fees and transport fares as the Archdiocese had not officially approved my study and had not accepted me as a student for Priesthood. It cost me thousands of dollars and I didn't have any employment. The government allowed me a small study allowance. I was grateful the church authority fed and housed me. Once again, I was totally reliant on others for the basics of my existence as I had in earlier times and in different places.

Chapter 11
St Patrick's Manly

Impressive! The physical size, the form and historical significance of the main building - Moran House - was awe-inspiring, pure and simple. Though the building was pure and simple in its inspiration, that which happened within was far from pure and simple.

Real estate! The Catholic Archdiocese of Sydney owns the several hectares of prime land situated on top of the northern Headland of Sydney Harbour. It has sweeping views of the Harbour itself, the ocean beach of Manly and its promenade of tall pine trees and rear vistas out as far as one can see across the roaring, turbulent, dark and threatening Pacific Ocean. The sea which formed the headlands, bashed them into steep sandstone cliffs. The sea which invades the harbour toward The Bridge and Sydney Opera House. The sea which forms the best harbour in the world, site of the first European settlement of the Great Southern Land, Terra Australis, the largest island on the Planet.

Grandeur! The edifice of Moran House - better known in the community as

Saint Patrick's College - can be seen from parts of the city and from along the coastal fringe of the northern beach side suburbs of Sydney and from vantage points along the harbour shores itself. It features on post cards and tourist information the world over.

Such was the building within which I would live, move and have my being for the next three years, those of my late thirties. One quiet afternoon in January 1993 I arrived, collected my key and settled into my room many metres above ground level, several 100m above sea level. I could gaze beyond the pine trees which lined Manly Ocean Beach across to the next headland, Queenscliff. From the broad black and white tiled veranda outside my window I could enjoy views of Manly below, the ocean to the right and greater Sydney to the left. I could hear fog horns of great ships, tugs and ferries navigating the Harbour.

A secular observer may say I had it made. I hadn't. I was on the bottom of the heap. I was a first-year seminarian. Life beyond this first year was to have run as follows: four or more years as a student of Theology, a year or more of placement in a parish, ordination to the Diaconate more years in placement, ordination to the priesthood, several years as an assistant priest then the possibility of further ministry as a Parish Priest (PP) being responsible for the pastoral care of a community, responsible for the financial management and stewardship of property and other parish community assets, employment of parish staff and other responsibilities as directed by the Archbishop of Sydney. All that without a physical life partner as a single and celibate chaste man living, often alone, in a dark cold presbytery.

Despite my years and life experience, as a person on the autism spectrum I could not see my future beyond that room with a view and my theological studies at Manly. The years ahead were to be challenging in many ways. I was to discover so much about the inner life of the Church, the lives of those of the Clerical State, the truth of Biblical Scripture, the sadness of life, the joys, the mysteries of faith, mysteries of belief, mysteries in the teaching and practice of church. All that and more.

Several months earlier: in the secure office of His Eminence Cardinal Clancy Archbishop of Sydney - I was announced by Michael Foster and introduced then sat opposite the eminent one at his oversized desk. A desk which was reminiscent of that which was used by the Most Reverend Founder Superior General of the Society of St Gerard Majella - Brother John Sweeney SSG. (Where do these people get such titles?) Cardinal Clancy was not a man of words, rather one of high authority. We had met earlier at Epiphany House where I carried his Holy Water and turned the pages in his ritual book, though

I am not sure he remembered me several months later. I mentioned that I had worked with his brother Ken at Chevalier, but the big man seemed to glaze over at my oblique reference which was out of context. He did smile somewhat though. Cardinal Clancy gripped my hand and said, 'Welcome aboard Paul." I wondered what ship we were aboard and where we would sail and if the seas would be calm or stormy and if Jesus was asleep in the stern of the boat while the storm raged around us. I had more to say than he: "Thank you your Eminence, Have a good afternoon." He nodded and I strode out with clammy hands as Michael called "next please" to the courier driver in a fashion not too dissimilar to a man named Stephen some twenty years earlier in another corridor in another church institution.

    At the age of 14 or 15 when I was a fresh innocent altar boy at St Andrew's Malabar the assistant priest, Fr John Sullivan sort of latched on to me and asked my parent's permission to take me to the football at Cronulla. It was the occasion of the first limited tackle league games at that oval. Not sure if we went several times to the footy but I do remember feeling honoured and special being with him. *Sull*, as he was known, was on the seminary staff as a spiritual guide. A reunion of sorts, the altar boy joins the seminary to train as a priest.

It may have been said that almost any priest living in any part of the State of New South Wales, especially any Sydney Priest, must have studied for a time, at St Patricks. Most diocese across the State didn't have their own Seminary so all students came to Sydney to live on the hill. They came from as far afield as Wilcannia-Forbes, Maitland-Newcastle, Wollongong, Armidale, Lismore and Wagga Wagga not to forget the other Sydney metropolitan diocese of Parramatta and Broken Bay. Indeed, the Manly Headland was itself surrounded by parishes of the diocese of Broken Bay. When greater Sydney was broken into three Diocese a dark red line marked to perimeter of the Manly estate indicating that, though it lay nowhere near the city of Sydney, the Seminary and the Catholic Institute of Sydney were governed under the control of the Archdiocese. St Pat's Manly was the 'spiritual' home for hundreds of 'brother' Priests across the State. They all had their stories, tales and memories of their own 'Manly Days'. Many thousands more who began or 'passed through' Manly and had not continued to Ordination, or who had for some reason left the priesthood, they too had their memories, fond or not so fond. Some former Manly men went on to become Bishops, or Cardinals. One by the name of Tony Abbott became the Australian Prime Minister not so long ago. At the time of writing, he still frequented the local beach wearing brief red swimwear and when required fights bush fires in summer.

Oh, I studied there for four years in total, including the year I lived at Epiphany House, my first year as a Seminarian in Moran House and two years in the ugly brick block of Kelly House. My favourite subjects at the Institute were: Biblical Studies, Philosophy, Pastoral Counselling, Church History and Liturgy while those I endured were Ancient Greek and least of all Latin. Human formation - no it was more Clerical Formation, took place on weekends and after hours. We learnt singing in choir, ok, the others learnt singing, I was flat most of the time and half a bar behind the others as I failed to read ahead. We had one or two sessions on Marriage facilitated by Vince Casey the Rome trained psychologist accompanied by two young recently married lovers who would have been better off finding a room than sitting gazing into each other's eyes for an hour as they whispered under moaning breath about the glories of the sacred physical union of one man and his wife. Nothing was said of the single life we were expected to lead, a life dedicated to the church as Bride of Christ a life of total physical abstinence in solemn chastity and under a Vow of Celibacy. One student told me he was going to spiritually marry Jesus! He went on to be assistant to the archbishop at St Marys Cathedral.

Nothing was said of Sexual abuse by Clergy on Children and vulnerable adults in our care. Nothing but whispers in the corridors when a certain 'alleged' paedophile priest, Fr Peter Lewis Comensoli came to visit on 'study leave'. He looked like a creep a big fat greasy priest. He was avoided in the library, ignored at the dining table and we averted our eyes as we passed him. The Study Leave would have been a period while out on bail with conditions not to reside in Wollongong or be near children.

> *"In the Sydney District Court on 18 October 1994, Father Peter Lewis Comensoli (then aged 55, of the Wollongong diocese, south of Sydney) was sentenced to 24 months jail (18 months minimum) after pleading guilty to the indecent assault of altar boys. His conviction was reported in Sydney and Wollongong newspapers."*
> *http://www.brokenrites.org.au/drupal/node/194*

Later during my time at Manly it, for some reason, became necessary for Fr Rector - Paul McCabe to issue an edict that any seminarian found in possession of condoms would be immediately requested to leave, return home, report to his local bishop and would not be considered for ordination or re-entry to the Seminary for a period to be determined. Why would a good Catholic man be in possession of condoms unless he was engaging in sexual activity with another person? Were some having sex with women in the wider community? Perhaps some were homosexual. Perhaps there existed the forbidden 'particular friendships' within the St Patrick's institution. Heaven forbid! We were permitted to have friends but not 'particular' friends. The fear of 'particular' friendships was that two would become close, perhaps close enough to have emotional attachments expressed physically. We had to be chaste not chased. In any case, no condoms. I secretly purchased some from vending machines in pub toilets and hid them in my room on the off chance the Rector would spring a random condom inspection and so I would have to leave the place! He never raided rooms. I remained a couple of years beyond the condom ban.

At one time I was called to the office of the 1st year moderator Fr Paul Monkerud. He wanted to discuss my behaviour and experience as a first-year seminarian. Apparently, something had caught his attention and he asked about the 'Easter egg incident'. This confirmed the strongly held rumour that the archdiocese kept a secret dossier on each of us. The conversation was honest but awkward on both sides. Why did I choose to break the egg in that manner, what was I feeling at the time, was I feeling the same then as I did last Tuesday at 9:08pm outside the tearoom? Did the authorities keep a diary or secret dossier, who had access to the personal files, might this 'egg incident' cloud my future as a priest of the archdiocese of Sydney? No wonder I ran down to catch the first available ferry into the city on a Friday night and return by the last ferry back. I had to get out of there but felt a 'calling' a Vocation from God to minister as a Priest in the church of Sydney.

During the semester breaks of my second and third years I was assigned to parishes to experience life with the priests. Oh, here are some stories. The locations and names will be withheld for privacy.

An inner-city parish with chaplains to the local hospital. My activity each day but Sunday was to check in to the chaplaincy office and study the lists of recent admissions for patients identified as RC, then plan rounds of Ward visits for the morning and afternoon trying to say hello and offer Holy Communion and prayers to the new ones. Then back to the priests' house for meals. In the evening I'd write up my concerns and learnings for the day. One cold evening the assistant priest invited me out for a walk for 'fresh air'. I asked why we couldn't speak in a room such as the front parlour. He said he preferred the fresh air. So, I followed him into the nearby parkland. As my dear friend Martha said prophetically years before, all will be revealed. The junior priest revealed that the senior PP had listening devices planted in key areas including the kitchen and dining rooms and the front parlour. I was assured that the bedrooms didn't have cameras fitted, to his knowledge.

An eastern suburban parish on the coast. The priests there specialised in home visitations and I had to accompany the PP on his rounds of the parish. One afternoon we parked outside a house and walked up to the front door and rang the bell. Soon we heard acknowledgement there were people at home: "Mum, the bloody priest is at the door!" Silence. Maybe they thought we'd go away. The bloody priest persisted arrogantly ringing the bell despite my encouragement to move along. "Tell him your mum isn't home." "I think they heard us mum." "Oh drat". We hear footsteps approaching. Door opens. "oh, hello Father, come in have a seat. Would you like a cup of tea?" I managed to stare at the carpet and sip the tea for half an hour. We then left and went up the road to the Naval base - HMAS Watson which fell within the parish boundaries. The priest obviously felt he had jurisdiction being the catholic priest of the area. I said they probably won't let us in, he persisted and drove right up to the boom gate to be greeted by a tall defence person who asked for ID for both of us and enquired as to our reason for entry. The priest simply said he was the Parish Priest and I was a seminarian and that he wished to show me the ocean view from the back of the military facility. The guard smiled and explained that we couldn't gain access without an appointment and written permission from his commanding officer. As we drove back to the presbytery, I felt so embarrassed for the mum and boy and that the priest believed he had the right to just rock up to a private home or a military institution and insist by his very presence that he be admitted, no questions asked. No wonder he and his companion priest spent their evenings alone on the couch watching tv dramas and drinking good whisky. I avoided that every night but one when they insisted, I join them. After an hour I was off to bed. The other nights I'd do the washing up and scrub the grimy lard encrusted kitchen after doing my best to digest the defrosted lump of food left in the deep freezer by the housekeeper, before trotting off to my room.

    A southern coastal parish near a national park. Priest left the answering machine on and only responded to calls at his discretion. Life as a priest was meant to be happy and enjoyed while offering care to those in need. This priest rarely sat at home drinking, let alone eating defrosted meals. No. He arranged to eat out most nights, either in the home of a family - usually a widow or poor single woman because they needed male company - or at a restaurant, because hard working priests deserved to dine on good food. It was arranged I dine with one such widow who prepared a beautiful spaghetti bolognaise with hand grated parmesan cheese. I did prefer to eat at home even if I had to cook it myself.

I managed to avoid these parish placements for the summer of 1994'95 by suggesting a placement with a charity. That year I worked at an inner suburban Vinnies shop. I sometimes sorted the donations, but mostly was on the truck as the offsider. The driver was a big strong Māori man with a long ponytail. He was tough, not necessarily a practicing catholic but a kind man. I developed muscles like I had never had before as if I were a gym fanatic pumping iron each day. I also developed a deeper understanding of inner suburban life and learnt how to load a truck with furniture. Close to 20% of clothing donations were sent to the paper factory to be shredded and processed into glossy magazines. Some of the furniture was taken directly to the tip too. A real eye opener. It wasn't all in the lower socioeconomic areas though. One afternoon we had a call to pick up a leather lounge. It was in the 'shed' or games room beside the pool area. We lifted the lounge above the full-sized snooker table and headed to the truck which was parked near a Lamborghini. The lady of the house asked us not to carry the lounge over the car and to be careful of the Lamborghini. I asked, "the red one?" yes, she said.

It was on that Vinnies truck that I heard over the radio of the charges and sentencing against Br Stephen Robinson, Br Joseph Pritchard and Br John Sweeney SSG. The realisation swept over me like a tsunami. I felt as if I was drowning in the revelation, the realisation that the decades of holding them as cherished men of the church had vanished and the stark light of day hit me as if emerging from a cave. I had to tell someone. I told Vince Casey as soon as I got back home to Manly. Vince listened to my full account of what happened to me during my year with the Brothers of St Gerard and with Stephen Robinson in particular. I too was one of his victims of what we now name as Clerical Sexual Abuse. I felt that while Vince listened, the outpouring of my emotional story of abuse and false trust I was not helped at all. I felt deep anger, grief, sadness, frustration. I felt neglect, violation, loss of faith in some clerics - priests and brothers and sisters too. Though I still clung onto the belief that basically all clerics were good people. It was the abuse of trust, the abuse of my trust in a 'holy' man, Stephen Robinson, that damaged me the most. We still celebrated Eucharist singing his hymns and the Mass for Moderns. Stephen was a brilliant liturgical musician, a grand organist a writer of inspirational songs and music, one looked up to in the wider church community of Sydney and Australia. He was in jail Guilty of sexual assault of a minor, a fellow 'brother' of the Society of St Gerard Majella - patron saint for the protection of children and young people. My second name, given by my dear parents for my spiritual protection was Gerard! From that time, I declined to use it as a name. A month later, one evening, I took my friend the former courier driver to a quiet place at the front of Moran House where I asked him to watch as I let my anger out. I took some old sandstone in my bare hands and smashed it against a tree trunk. I smashed it and smashed it again till it was pummelled into fine sand and my body was exhausted. My friend looked on in fear as if I had smashed Stephen Robinson's frail body to splinters of bone on those rocks. That's what I felt like doing, though I wouldn't carry it out. I left all that there, not addressing it for another several years.

Moving out of Manly

In 1995, the Seminary celebrated its closure due to a move, eventually, to an inner western Sydney suburb at Homebush. There were many celebrations, speeches, dinners and farewell events. Once again, I got to escort Cardinal Clancy around lest he be lost. One Saturday a few of us escaped the hype for a day heading out on the bay for fishing and a meal of roasted chicken and beer. No fish were caught but it was good to get away for a few hours. Another event was a lunch on the front porch of Moran house which was reported in the local paper! However, my favourite afternoon was acting as a parking marshal in the grounds directing priests and visitors from all over Sydney to a parking space in a far-flung corner giving them exercise which we thought was needed due to their lifestyle. Some felt they were more important than others and 'requested' a spot closer to the entrance. My answer to that attitude was "Oh sorry Father, we're expecting a few Cardinals to arrive soon and park there." They backed off.

Having given careful consideration to my time at Manly, the various experiences of living with Priests, and other turmoils within myself - I came to the decision that life in Ordained Ministry as a Catholic priest was not for me. I met with my supervisors and the spiritual guide as I came to that decision. Some staff suggested I stay for one more semester at the Institute and Seminary giving me the opportunity to complete a full session of Clinical Pastoral Studies. That, they suggested, may give me formal qualifications in Pastoral Ministry and I could secure employment in that field. I said I'd consider the option although I knew immediately that would be cheating, they system. I told them the next morning that I had decided to go and could not honestly take diocesan funds as a Seminarian and pretend to be such for another period. They understood. Meanwhile I did stay out the final few weeks as we all packed up for the big move.

Personally, the most poignant moment was the handing in of our keys while gathered by the bubble-wrapped statue of old St Patrick. I had my last backpack by my side having packed up everything the week before. Five minutes later I was in my mate's car with several others as he joyfully honked the horn and drove out the back gates and down Darley Road for the final time. I was out of there and soon on the Manly Ferry to Circular Quay and then the train to Bardwell Park and a walk up the hill to Epiphany House. There I packed my remaining belongings at the same time applying to study at the Australian Catholic University. I had a Bachelor of Theology but that was not going to be any good in the secular environment, so I enrolled in a Graduate Diploma in Adult and Community Education which occupied the academic year 1996. I was a Seminarian no more.

Chapter 12
Late 20th Century

The 1996 Atlanta Olympics were on and I bought a second-hand TV for the occasion. What I remember most was the traffic chaos and athletes and spectators delayed on buses and roads. My home was a flat, the front few rooms of a family home. They had extended at the rear with a new kitchen and separated the two parts with a wall. I had three rooms and paid the rent fortnightly in person at the back door. My studies continued at nearby Strathfield campus and my old Amstrad laptop, all 11 kilos of it, was perched on one side the kitchen table. On the first of April 1996 I began work with a Catholic agency in Polding House, the HQ in the city. I was to develop a 'pilot' program for ministry to Catholic high school children who attended State Schools, the rationale being that this cohort missed out on SRE - Special Religious Education in public schools. In the office I didn't announce or make it known that I had recently left the seminary. I wanted to distance myself and move on. I had been interviewed and hired by the Director of the agency, one Fr Richard. Two weeks later I recognised the next new employee a woman by the name of Jennifer Herrick. She also recognised me as she was being introduced around the office of 5 or 6 staff. Jennifer leant on my office door with a grin of familiarity as we had shared a Liturgical Music class at Manly. I indicated to her to be quiet about our earlier contact at Manly and arranged to share afternoon coffee with her at a local café. Jennifer kept my secret and we were soon sharing an office and lunches on days she happened to be in the city. I was there 4 days a week and she 2, but not on a regular schedule. As we had both been hired by Richard and our projects overlapped somewhat, we did some work together and shared resources. Our workplace friendship soon extended beyond the office; we enjoyed each other's company.

Meanwhile, for reasons unknown to us in the office, and probably kept that way, one afternoon Richard took the lift to level 13 to visit his boss, Cardinal Clancy. Fifteen minutes later Richard returned to the office in a plain business shirt, not his clerical attire. He had this to say: "Attention everyone. I have just been upstairs and handed in my collar, phone and told him where he can shove his keys. (the office was struck dumb, he finished with: "It's been good working with you. All the best." With that he left the building walking into Pitt Street, never to be seen again.

Several weeks later a new manager arrived from Queensland, apparently no one in Sydney, indeed in NSW, was qualified or no one wanted to work in that office under the command of he who occupied level 13. The new man was directed to cut costs in the office so one fateful Thursday I was called to his office and told I had two weeks to justify my work there as under the contract set by Richard or resign. As I left the office, I was asked to call Jennifer in. I must have looked pale and the others noticed. I was close to tears. Jennifer emerged five minutes later and had the same expression. We left the office shortly after having tidied my desk. I wanted to visit the chapel on level 2 but it was closed. That was a turning point in my spiritual journey. The catholic HQ had told me to go and didn't offer any support, not even the chapel was available. I took my prayers to the Uniting Church next door. I also took my car keys and drove for most of the two weeks clocking up almost 10,000 km on the 'company car'. I could use the vehicle for personal use as well as church use. Upon return I parked it in the basement and handed in the keys to the clerk. I then wrote emails to all my contacts saying I was finishing that day due to the new Director and the Cardinal not having the vision which Richard had when he employed me. I then deleted all my files on both my hard drive and the server before I left the building.

Just five months after we had announced our engagement and five months prior to our Nuptials, Jennifer and I were suddenly both out of work. I joined a hospitality agency and found some casual jobs as a function waiter at some clubs and private events.

Our plans for the wedding went ahead despite the unfortunate employment situation. Much of the preparations were carried out over the phone with me in my flat and Jennifer in hers 20 kilometres away. Meanwhile, she was completing her Master Honours in Theology considering the question "Does God Change?". We married on the 4th of March 1997 at Harbord Catholic Church with family, friends and parishioners attending the church ceremony and eighty of our closest at the reception. My friend the courier driver was one of the witnesses and organist along with a few other formal witnesses. Following a quiet honeymoon in Vanuatu which included a near drowning of the new groom, I moved into Jennifer's unit near Manly for the next year till we moved away from Sydney.

Our new home was in the beach side town, Umina, on the NSW Central Coast just north of Sydney and south of Newcastle. The house was almost new, only a few years old with an established lawn and garden. Jennifer and I planted fresh bushes and flowers, cut down three palm trees and a pine tree, and installed a rainwater tank to water the garden. Our furniture was blended, not that I had much really but we made the new house our home. Jennifer continued her academic career firstly studying Tourism at TAFE before taking on her PhD. Our most frequent visitor was Jen's mother Gwen who visited each Christmas and Easter and other times during the year. Others visited only once from Sydney claiming that the Hawkesbury River was such a deep physical divide between them and us. We visited them for birthdays and anniversaries several times a year and each time they asked where we were staying as it was so far. Each time we told them it's only an hour and a half drive back and we preferred to stay in our own bed. Sydney people were so reluctant to visit, apart from family.

Over a period of several years, we drifted from the Catholic Church to the Anglican where we became quite involved including in the liturgy and parish events. After some years we moved away from regular practice of church attendance altogether while remaining close to the catholic church and keeping friends with an Anglican family we met at Gosford.

I had since started a new job as Pastoral Care Coordinator at a Catholic Retirement Village in Sydney. It was only 30 hours a week which I spread over five days. It was a busy but satisfying job. However, my contract was not renewed after 24 months due to staff restructuring. An elderly retired religious Sister took my place somewhat to the dismay of most residents who, being 'lay' people, related better to a married man than a 'nun'. My farewell afternoon tea planned for half a dozen corporate staff expanded into a full-blown event with scores of residents attending. They streamed up to the timbered grand dining room arriving on foot, pushing trollies, walkers, in wheelchairs and on disability lounges. We had to call down to the kitchen for more sandwiches and fried finger food and urns of hot water for tea and coffee. The manager had to set out chairs and tables as the multitudes arrived. Nursing staff were assigned to care for those who were in need, reception and accounting staff served drinks while kitchen staff cleaned up afterwards. It was the best farewell ever, so much love in the room among the people who mattered. It was a classic look of chagrin on the faces of management who had just got rid of me. I left that afternoon with a sad heart but with determination to move on to a new occupation.

By now it was the Turn of the Century. A new millennium was upon us!

The period of the 9-11 attacks in September 2001 punctuated life for a moment, everyone was affected in some way. I stayed up late that night watching the towers fall to the streets of New York. I had to face work the next day and my classes at the University of Sydney Foundation Program. My students were in shock asking me to try to explain how it could have happened. We all felt quite numb. This event changed how we live in daily life from airport security to anti-tampering devices on food containers and heightened awareness of personal and community security.

My usual occupations around this time included a mix of hospitality work and adult education with a focus on English for speakers of other languages. At the University of Technology, Sydney (UTS), I studied a Graduate diploma in TESOL while teaching at Gosford TAFE but as I was not officially qualified, the TAFE saw it their duty to let me go after almost two years of teaching service. The next year I sat on the other side of the desk doing a certificate in Hospitality. I learnt 'front of house' skills including wine appreciation, table service, how to be a Maître D, Bar and Barista skills. Later, I was the highest qualified and most underpaid dishwasher and waiter around.

As the twentieth Century drew to a close and fears of Y2K came and went, so our marriage rolled on too. We had our joys and difficulties unique to our relationship.

The undercurrent or at least one of the main ones of our married life was my sexuality and the emotional conflict surrounding it. I had always had an attraction to males. When I was younger in my twenties I was attracted to men of a similar age. Being married to a woman was a major problem. Marriage in a traditional understanding of that institution which in 1996 was the only option for marriage.

I didn't dare choose a man and move in with him and live a secret life. I had tried that in the early 1980s with John. He and I never declared our love for each other, nor did we publicly declare or say we were a 'couple'. Though several around us knew but never said anything till one afternoon at my parent's place when they invited me to an outing or something and I said I'd have to check with John. Mum said directly to me "It's not as if you are joined at the hip." Nothing further was said. I left the country, went to PNG for three years and returned to take up my job with

Australia Post as if nothing had happened. Then life evolved as you have read.

Having lived in unhealthy psychological denial for decades, including going off to two monasteries, The Mission field, doing church work in different places and spending four years in an institution studying theology planning a single chaste life as a Priest; by the time I was in my early forties I was: single, and still attracted to men but also still frightened to admit it. One night in a park near home I took a clear decision that traditional marriage was the only option. To pretend, yet again, but on a permanent basis that I was 'normal'. I secretly believed that marriage to a woman would 'cure' me or marriage would be my 'gay behaviour therapy'. It wasn't electrodes attached to my scrotum, as a mate had done to himself in the 70s, nor was it chemical treatment, nor psychological treatment imposed by others. In effect, it was a self-imposed psychosocial exile from reality. Being a person with undiagnosed Asperger syndrome on the Autism Spectrum, I had no concept of the ramifications or consequences this decision would have on any future wife, let alone on my mental health. My only focus in early 1996 was to try to be seen and accepted as 'normal'. I wanted my brother and sisters, my parents and others to believe I was simply a usual run of the mill heterosexual male. As a gay man I felt unaccepted, looked down upon by society, my beloved church, fellow students, work mates, people in the street. I feared others 'knowing' the truth about me, feared them judging me by my appearance, my walk, or glance, my fashion choices. At school aged 14 or 15 I was singled out by an older woman history teacher who checked fingernails and hand hygiene in class. She inspected the boys' hands and I was made to stand up and show the others how neat my nails were and my soft clean hands. At church and school, I was known as the altar boy, in my young adult years I was known as the Acolyte. Probably seen as one who was somewhat effeminate or 'less masculine' than others. My favourite sports position was 'left right out'. Not really. I felt left out and shunned. The 'real' or masculine boys played football or cricket or were muscular due to swimming. I wanted to put all that behind me and for once be a normal masculine Australian male. If I was married, I didn't have to prove myself in other ways such as playing sport or working in a physically tough trade. Marriage was the golden seal of normality!

    Marriage itself didn't cure my homosexual attraction to other men. The sexual attraction remained however, I did not act on it beyond thinking of possibilities, dreaming and gazing longingly at images of attractive men. At one stage I did chat online with other men about my sexual attractions and dreams. This period was one of extreme tension and anxiety between us and within my being. It involved many medical appointments and consultations with psychologists and sexual health specialists. Life between us as a couple was very difficult at times. Apart from my social and mental health the psychological effects spilled over into my work environment causing, no doubt, workplace tension and impacted performance and often difficult behaviour. My resume extended to several pages showing what a marketing person would gloss as: "great versatility in job skills and ability to adapt" but a competent manager or HR person would read: "lack of ability to focus and keep a job beyond several months and unable to work appropriately in a team environment, or as exhibiting volatile and at times inappropriate work place behaviour and practice". I felt trapped in a marriage which didn't match my sexuality, sexual preference nor my personality. I was putting on a face of heterosexual normality as if a clown hiding terror deep within.

Interlude.

In the middle of all this the Global Financial Crisis hit Australia in 2008-09. I had an opportunity to seek a break from the domestic scene and take a job overseas. The choice was China or Korea.

Chapter 13
China 中国 or Korea 대한민국?

While teaching English to international students in Sydney in 2007 to 2008, the GFC hit the world economy spreading across the USA to other Western Nations and their trading partners. Thanks to the new Kevin Rudd led Labor government in Australia certain financial strategies were implemented which 'saved' the nation from financial ruin such as that seen across Europe in that continent's 'austerity measures. In our small education institution in the city of Sydney, enrolments continued to be strong several months well into the GFC. We staff remained confident that the Crisis would pass us by, and we were safe and secure in employment. That turned out not to be the case!

Enrolments declined leading to staff being put off as we were all casual employees. I could see the writing on the wall. Classes closing, fewer students arriving and more leaving. Chinese, South Korean, Vietnamese, Thai, Columbian, Indian, wherever they came from were simply not spending thousands of Dollars to come to Sydney to live and learn English. They couldn't afford it. Jobs were lost. I joined several international English Teacher Job search sites. Any Native English Speaker from the UK, USA, Canada, NZ with any bachelor's degree could apply. I had an education degree specialising in Adult Education, so I had a greater chance to grab a job in this lucrative industry. The only catch was I'd have to live overseas and go to where the students were. Follow the demand. I had discussed this with Jennifer, and we thought it better I go and work overseas and get an income than struggle as a casual waiter clearing tables for $15 an hour.

I was accepted by an institution in the northern Chinese city of Jilin, to the north of North Korea and south of Russia at [43.8379° N, 126.5496° E].

My passport was lodged with the Chinese Consulate office in Sydney and arrangements had been made for flights to Jilin via Beijing. The family gathered for a farewell lunch, mum and dad and all the siblings attended. Farewells were said and my sister Cath gave me a thick pair of red woollen socks 'because it's cold there' she said. Walking back to the train behind dad and Jennifer I heard him ask "Jen, why is Paul doing this?" to which she responded, "I don't know Lloyd." However, it was clear to me that I needed a job, and this was the only opportunity I could see at the time. I was the husband and the man had to provide. This notion had been part of my social fabric ever since I noticed gender roles, it was reinforced at the height of the bush fire emergency of '06-'07 when Jennifer, her mother and I evacuated from a threatening blaze when Gwen said to Jen to tell Paul that he had to stay behind and defend the house. I was absolutely focussed on going to China I couldn't understand dad's question, nor why Jen didn't know.

Came the day to collect my Visa and pay for my ticket, then I would say my goodbyes to family and friends for two years in China. Jen was up early on her computer researching the school where I was to teach and before I could jump in the shower called me with some sound of alarm and urgency in her voice. She had been up since 3am and discovered many worrying accounts and reports of misadventure had by others who had applied to or who had turned up at the institution in Jilin. None were positive to say the least. Some escaped with what they could carry. The institution was a scam. I quickly washed and gobbled down some cereal and we dashed down the Pacific Highway for the city. Jen dropped me off at the consulate entrance and parked down the street. Many people were milling around the entrance, most like myself holding green receipts for our passports. A guard or consulate staff person pointed to his watch saying the office would close at 12:00noon. We all complained that we had valid receipts and that the closure had not been publicised. I was informed that a shop opposite may be able to assist me in my case as it was known to distribute passports by Post on behalf of the consulate. I located the yellow shop front. Inside was one woman behind a counter. Also, a glass display cabinet which held two bars of soap, a tube of toothpaste, and a box of aspirin as if it were out of stock. Four plain kitchen style chairs lined the window. The woman asked what I wanted as if I were to ask for the last toothpaste! I said I was told she could help me obtain my passport. She asked my name and searched through a large hand full of passports of a variety of nations. Mine wasn't there and halfway through addressing me in English she called speaking Mandarin to someone and I took a seat. Meanwhile Jennifer called asking where I was. I told her in the shop opposite. Where was she? Inside the consulate as she had told the guard that her husband was inside, so she was let in. Jen asked why I was at the little shop, but I told her I couldn't explain at the moment but to come over. At that time a man in a dark suit entered with envelopes stuffed with even more foreign passports. Simply carried across the street! The woman told me the 'special delivery service would cost me $20 cash, but she was interrupted by the man and then informed me that she was informed that the fee had increased to AU$50 for over-the-counter immediate delivery, otherwise I'd have to wait a week or more for delivery by mail at an extra charge. I handed over the $50 cash and without any receipt or check of ID received my passport. Presently, Jen arrived and asked what was going on. I said, 'walk with me back to the car and I'll explain on the way'. Just then the aforesaid man strolled up behind me and walked on my right and spoke into my ear as if a deep secret, and it was, 'this is a special service for you today only and do not tell others.' I said I understood, and he disappeared into the nearest lane way never to be seen again. We soon found the car and drove off to safety, but first had a brief stop into the travel agency where I cancelled my travel arrangements. We were safely home for a late lunch, feeling relieved though still somewhat anxious. Without delay, I called a contact in Foreign Affairs in Canberra who said she would 'inform the China Desk immediately'. The next day I cancelled my passport and applied for a fresh one.

That week I was contacted by The Canadian Connection based in Toronto who were the official agent for recruiting English teachers for South Korea. The had proven and verified credentials. After the appropriate processing and interviews I was approved and in a few weeks collected my Visa to teach English in Korea. I booked my ticket and was off for Seoul a week later.

Orientation was held in the regional city of Gwangju. A week later I was on my way to Wando Island where I took up residence and taught English in the state government High School.

Wando High school educated students from grades 9 to 12. They learnt subjects including Mathematics, Science,

Chinese, Asian History, Korean language including Hangul (한글) the script, and played sports including basketball, volleyball, football (Soccer) and gymnastics. These subjects accounted for 90% of their total assessment while English was part of the remaining 10% along with: class behaviour, uniform, neatness, politeness, basic sewing for boys and girls and personal hygiene. On a national and provincial level, English was compulsory in the education curriculum, but it counted as less than 1% resulting in the attitude: "this is Korea, we speak Korean, we don't need to learn English." The attitude was held and expressed by the Principal, his Vice Principal and most of the teachers. Even my co-teacher of English told me English is seen as a bit more than an entertainment and at most a period of one hour a week when the students can relax from the stress of other more valued subjects. Till then I was tense and anxious in class and way too serious. I began to relax and entertain in English with role plays and fun classes which included mood lighting and music and some back-row dancing to ABBA and the local Wonder Girls.

    Wando town was the administrative and commercial centre of Wando Provence and Wando Island was the largest of 200 islands in the Provence. The island could be circumnavigated by the only main road in about 20 minutes by car, or 30 mins by bus. There is a regular ferry service to some outlying islands while some are close enough to be linked by bridge.

My apartment was on level 14, with a view across the carpark to the other apartment buildings in the complex of five blocks. One small grocery store sold basic supplies, otherwise I went shopping at the town supermarket 'Chang Pogo Mart'. Above the local shop was a chicken restaurant which I visited often of a Friday night for the best fried chicken and litre of refreshing beer. Also, in town were several other speciality shops, local Korean fast-food restaurants, a Chinese restaurant, heaps of family run seafood restaurants, music rooms (노래방, no rae bang) (karaoke style), bars and scores of saunas known as JimJil (찜질방). (Travelers or backpackers' hostel) and their associated and more common Mok York Tang (목욕탕) (bathroom / sauna).

The Wando Hotel Café hosted the fortnightly English language social group. This had been meeting for several years with members including local Korean English speakers and we the teachers. Each time we enjoyed hazelnut coffee which seemed to be the only variety served. Sadly, these few people were in the minority of those who spoke English in the Provence. Shopping and basic activities such as attending the hospital or pharmacy or buying coffee and pastry were much more difficult than I had ever experienced in other countries. Many signs and other information had English language as well as Korean but that didn't mean the people spoke or read English. I read: hospital, pharmacy, bank, post office, police, supermarket, bus station, hairdresser, coffee shop and ferry wharf. Thank goodness for globalization, most grocery items had pictures or were categorised in their aisles. It was also a great assistance that banking and paying bills was automated, though in Korean, I was able to complete transactions by literally remembering patterns on the screens. Once I needed a doctors' prescription for cholesterol medication. I went into the clinic which was indicated by a green cross. I asked the receptionist for an appointment, but he couldn't speak English enough to help so he called his brother in Seoul who had lived in Brisbane a few years earlier. So, I spoke to this man about my medical requirements, he translated this to his brother who spoke to the medical doctor who prescribed what I needed. The receptionist accompanied me to the pharmacy which was a great help. I took a photo of the clinic and showed my Korean friend who laughed, I had been to an orthopaedic specialist. From then on, I walked up to the hospital and took a number to be seen by a doctor who didn't speak English but who asked the cleaner to translate for us. After several months of requesting an English-speaking doctor, one was assigned to me.

He was a volunteer for two years due to his ethical objection to compulsory military service. This was one bright moment in my medical treatment while in Korea.

The mid-year holiday at school was scheduled for five weeks, during which period I would be paid as if on duty and working. What a deal, right? The teachers and students worked very long hours, the final year 12s often in attendance between 07:30 and 23:00. I listened intently to the principal's message on the Friday at end of term. Not that I understood a word, but it was translated for me. He wished all a good summer break beginning Monday. After fifteen minutes he gleefully said he was looking forward to seeing everyone fresh and bright on Wednesday morning from 8 o'clock. Yes. Two days off, then Summer School. The actual time off was the last of five weeks. All my English teacher colleagues had booked the five weeks off on international holidays to Vietnam and so on. I had booked week two to visit Japan. I read my contract which said I was allowed a full week out of the country during the summer break. Unfortunately, I didn't know I had to seek written permission from the principal to leave Korea. This was hastily arranged with the caveat that if required I could be recalled. I agreed on the assurance of others that it was a mere technicality. My trip to Japan is documented elsewhere.

It's the account of a visitor from China which was the most intriguing and alarming which I feel must be told before moving on. Why it's said to be alarming, I'll leave to you dear reader.

Remember I had plans to work in China, but they were dramatically cancelled? At that time, I was working in the city teaching mainly Chinese students who told me of the Chinese messaging and social website QQ.

I saw it as a challenge to set up my own QQ account though it was all in Mandarin script. How difficult could it be? One weekend I managed to create an account, create photo albums and upload photos of life in Australia such as kangaroos and the Sydney Opera House. I also set a profile picture of myself in a business shirt. Along with this I managed to set up a chat list as some people contacted me via QQ chat. There were a few regulars including a nurse, a teacher, and a few others who could at least write English and wanted to practice chatting in English with me, a native speaker. Of course, I announced I'd soon be off to teach in China which gained some interest. However, once I was accepted to go to Wando Korea, I bad farewell to my chat friends. That was it. No more China connection.

Meanwhile, back in Wando: Upon returning from a cross country visit to Busan I popped into the Samsung store in Wando where Josh worked. He was a regular at the English Coffee Club. I showed him my new second-hand phone which I had bought in Busan for AU$70. We exchanged phone numbers. I felt like I was more part of Korea having a local phone. Several days later I received a call on that phone, it was the waitress from the Wando Hotel saying a woman from Beijing just walked in asking for Paul from Australia! I was surprised on a few fronts. I asked the waitress how she got my number as I had only just got it. She said she knew me from the Coffee Club and knew Josh was a friend, so she asked him if he had my number, which he gave her. I wasn't too happy he gave it to her but she's ok. However, what about the mystery woman from Beijing?

Dear reader, here is a direct quote from my Korean Journey blog of 2009:

"So, I went to the coffee shop, cost about $2.50 by taxi or 30 mins walk in the sticky heat... got a taxi.

Arrived there and the waitress said the woman had just left and I could see her in her room. I told the waitress (who knows me a bit) that I'd see the woman here [at the café]. so soon she arrived. We took photos and had photos taken. I had coffee she didn't finish hers. a hazelnut cappuccino. what to do next??

I suggested a walk. she said it was too hot, that we could go to her room to watch TV. she headed off along the corridor and I said no. "I am not going to your room to watch TV." so she asked me *to sit on the lounge in the foyer. her oral English was not good. I insisted we go for a walk. So, we toured Wando on foot for 30 mins. We even found a Chinese restaurant, but the ladies spoke Mandarin for a while, and they decided I should go back to the Hotel. I took her to the supermarket and then to the Samsung shop. Then we went back toward the hotel and we had a buffet meal for $10 each. She paid. Good food. Then I said I had to go back and talk to my wife. I had mentioned that a few times along the way. She said, 'so you really like your wife." I said yes. Oh! she said. she asked if I was free tomorrow, we could go walking again. I said I was not sure what I'd be doing tomorrow. (Thus, not saying yes, we can do something~~) So she sadly said that in that case, she would head back to Seoul tomorrow. I told her how much to expect to pay for the taxi and the bus to Seoul. By this time, I think she took the hint!!*

We stepped outside the restaurant and I clearly said (with hand actions) "you go that way and I will go this way, Goodbye nice to have met you". We shook hands and said Goodbye.

I didn't look back.

I marched away and hailed the first taxi out of there."

That night in our regular Skype call, Jennifer listened intently and reinforced that I truly needed to be very careful in my communications over the internet and in my social behaviour. I did try my best.

However, the overall situation and circumstance was against me.

As is consistent with most of my working and private life, I had difficulties in that workplace. My main troubles were with the Principal and the Vice Principal, two strong authority figures. I was in a bad place socially, culturally and I didn't know the language. At least in PNG I knew the language and my place in the scheme of things. In Wando Korea I was totally out of my depth, drowning. Silent visits to the town Bath House and regular massage were my soul relief. I could relax and be myself in my own mind.

While I was attracted to men, I never acted on that attraction in my loyalty to Jennifer and our marriage. Two women did try to seduce me, one being the woman from Beijing, another being a friend of my massage therapist from the Bath House. He invited her to my 55th birthday party along with another married couple. After the dinner party, this woman suggested I would like a 'special and personal' massage with a 'happy ending' for my birthday! I told her I'm married but she said not to worry. I continued to say no, but she continued to try to get me. I then resorted to the bit of Korean I knew saying "*Shimsimhe*" 심심해 or 'boring'. She was shocked but I just had to get out of the situation and didn't know the polite language to express my thoughts and feelings.

As I say, there were struggles with the men in authority. One too many deep sincere apologies and I had to go. Meanwhile the six-month mark of my contract drew close, so I held on till then before asking release to return to Australia. Release was granted and I was soon packing up and, on my way, back to Sydney.

Return to Australia and moving out.
Following three nights in Bangkok I returned to my dear family home at Matraville where I waited another three days for Jennifer to come and take me home again to Umina Beach.

I was in the back room when she arrived at the front door greeting mum and dad with 'where is he?'. I felt in the wrong place, once again. I should have been waiting on the front veranda looking out for her arrival.

From then on, life between us seemed to me, to be different to before, I felt some unease for several months. We had been separated for both our birthdays and though we saw each other via video link, it wasn't the same as being together, hearing each other at home, going out for meals and visits to parks and all that. There was a gap in our common experience. All the photos and retelling of stories and experiences were experiences had alone. Gradually we came to build a fresh set of shared life experiences. The next few years were difficult in a range of ways, shared struggles which brought us closer but others which were more challenging. Jennifer's physical health with her limbs was a challenge which brought us closer, the same can be said of the challenge of her mother's old age and sad passing from this life. I struggled to secure employment in adult education and hospitality. I eventually became unemployable and was put on the Disability Pension.

    Crunch time hit us one afternoon and was to be the turning point in our relationship. I had a sorry habit of withdrawing to my room and shutting the door. This behaviour became more frequent and deeply depressing over a year or so. Each time Jennifer said she had a difficult time trying to handle this troublesome behaviour. Several times she said she couldn't handle it anymore but then we tried and tried to continue, not acknowledging the truth of the matter. Then that afternoon, Jennifer came to the room and leant on the doorway saying she simply couldn't take it anymore. I remarked she had said the same several times, but we had marched on. We had tried everything as I've said. We had a cup of tea and agreed that somehow, we needed to address the issue. After much prayer and many long conversations on the couch, we came to the decision to separate but remain married. I was to move out. We agreed upon it together. We looked around for a place I could live and focussed on self-care retirement villages in the local area. Being over 55 I was eligible. I picked one which I particularly liked due to the location and ethos. Together we looked at units and chose one near the rear fence in a quiet corner. Arrangements were made and I soon moved into unit 211. Anne and her family along with Jen helped me move in. Jennifer and I visited each other often over the years, she attended social functions at the Village and so on. However, after a year or so we agreed to make it official and signed divorce papers. The marriage ended. It was a difficult period for a while, but we clung to the vision of continuing as close friends into our future lives.

Chapter 14
Mental health and sexuality

This was the period between my return from Korea till our separation that Jennifer and I tried coming to grips with my mental state and the syndrome of Asperger on the Autism Spectrum. Jennifer was with me during many of my sessions with my psychologist who diagnosed me. The three of us worked together over a period of years on this and associated behaviour.

As I've said already, my sexuality and associated mental health are intertwined and intrinsic to my rich fabric of my being.

Sexuality

In the educated and experienced opinion of the psychologist, not only was I on the Autism Spectrum but on a point in the sexual preference spectrum or continuum as well.

Regarding my sexuality and sexual preference, I felt that I was about 30% along the continuum from the 'gay' or homosexual end till I was sexually abused by a male paedophile in my late teenage years. The psychologist said very clearly that the sexual abuse moved me along the continuum more towards the gay side. Jennifer listened carefully and respected her professional opinion.

This whole matter of sexuality needs to be 'unpacked' further.

These days some people ask, "When did you know you were Gay?" I find that question awkward to consider. It is a lifetime of becoming self-aware. Then there arrives a time or period when one can call oneself Gay.

When I was in second class at the age of 7, I was trapped by a sixth-class girl who grabbed my bag and bribed me to kiss her. Perhaps she was on natural hormones as her breast was well developed and I was a cute little boy. I hated it and washed my face and ran home immediately after the assault. I avoided her and other girls for years after that episode. At around the same age, still in primary school, I brought a boy named Steven home to see where I lived. I remember thinking he's so handsome and doesn't wear a singlet as we had to in our family. I felt jealous of him in some way. I was also attracted by the blond boy Warren who invited me to his 5th birthday party. He didn't wear a singlet either! Later in high school I was often caught staring at more handsome school mates, especially the swimmers and some of the footballers when they changed on the side of the footy field. At the age of 15, I went to boarding school at Mittagong as I've outlined earlier. It was such a hot house of teenage male testosterone. The tall year 12 student with thick blond hair, who was a favourite of the principal Brother Valerius, caught my eye too. He was given the privilege to use the chainsaw and I could see his bulging chest and arm muscles under his shirt. It was not an attraction acted upon though, simply good to look at kind of attraction as one may be attracted to a beautiful flower or a river in the countryside.

    All through life I've found certain men attractive to look at and observe. Once at a Canberra club on the way back to Sydney from a weekend in the Snowy mountains with the CYO group I noticed a tall blond hunky surfer type at a table near us. He was sitting with his girlfriend. He noticed I was looking his way and came across and accused me of looking at his girlfriend. He chased us out to the car park and threatened me with a tri-sided metal spike. Glad he didn't think I was checking him out!

There are other examples of such attraction, however these few are given here to highlight this theme.

Turning now to mental health.

As I've told you dear reader, it was in late 2009 upon my return from time in South Korea that I was formally diagnosed as an Aspie - A person within the Asperger Syndrome of the autism spectrum. High functioning Asperger's so they say. That means to the casual observer it would appear my behaviour or thought patterns were no different or not so dissimilar from 'normal' or 'neurotypical' people.

Some people said things such as "Paul is different", "Paul's like that", "just nod and say yes to Paul" "Paul is a bit strange", "He's slow", "He's very sensitive", "Paul's a slow learner", or in sporting situations I was picked last to join a team then given the position of 'left right out' or told not to touch the ball and so on.

As a young teen or adolescent, I was awkward socially. Dad told me to swing my arms like a man rather than clasp my hands behind my back when walking. Was that because I'm gay? I don't think he was thinking that, just trying to get me to fit in and look normal like others.

Education

At school I was fast getting through the reading laboratory tasks, faster than others in the class. I guess I could see patterns in the texts, I don't know. I've always usually found slabs of text difficult to comprehend and keep track of the meaning. I'd have to read over again before grasping the meaning. Once I had the meaning or understanding it was simple. The penny had dropped. However, because I took time to read over and over before understanding, I was 'slow' at learning. At high school I was in the mid-level grade. We had three tiers in high school. Black, Green and Gold. I was always in the Green level. When the education system changed in the mid-1960s under the Wyndham Scheme and years 11 and 12 were introduced, it was expected by my school community that the Black tier would all progress and eventually go to university. We in the middle may have had a chance at senior high school but would never be any good at university. The gold boys were expected to scrape through the school certificate in year 10 and then get a job digging roads and sweeping the gutters if they were lucky. This is a generalisation, but it may be seen in the context of my education. One or two of my teachers or others I held in high regard told me that I'd never complete the HSC let alone have a chance at university.

These people were Religious Brothers, my teachers, those who were to be respected and held in high esteem! They were right in one aspect; I never completed the HSC although I attempted twice. It was later in life that I completed a bachelor's degree in theology, a Graduate Diploma in Adult Education, another Graduate Diploma in TESOL and a Masters in TESOL. I have tutored Uni students at Notre Dame Sydney and taught Academic English to adults. Today, however, I still have dreams where I'm aged 60, with my master's but still in a year 12 HSC class trying to prove those naysayers wrong! Such was the effect of their opinions on my mental health.

Every person within Asperger Syndrome experiences life differently, the symptoms may be similar but not everyone has the same symptoms. I have difficulty reading text, trouble understanding drawn-out instructions, fail to follow stories and movie plots. I often miss social cues. I occasionally act inappropriately in situations. At times I think or believe that because something is usual in my experience that it is usual for all. I had the belief that all people were Catholic till I noticed children going to other schools, I asked Sister about them, she said they are 'Publics' because they go to public schools. I then categorised people into two groups – Catholics and Publics! Then one Sunday I asked dad about the man who sat in the car outside the church but never went into Mass. He had a goatee beard. Dad said he's an 'atheist', but I heard 'nudist', so I thought all men with goatees were nudists and weren't allowed into the catholic church. Obviously, I couldn't understand how a person could be atheist. Everyone believes in God, don't they? Were nudists atheists by default? I later discovered that a man can be nudist without a goatee beard and be a devout Christian.

Having touched on the aspects of sexuality and mental health, I shall now turn to Church and its response to sexual abuse by clergy.

Chapter 15
A challenging church!

All along, as I was trying to live with my sexual self and my autistic behaviour, I was struggling to cope with the sexual abuse by a cleric within the catholic church. Without covering the circumstances of that abuse here, mention needs to be made of the process which soon enveloped my life for years. The so called *Towards Healing* process of the Catholic Church and associated legalities and fallout or consequences.

I initiated the process in my first appointment with the lawyer Peter Karp at his Sydney office. Peter was all too sadly, aware of my 'alleged' abuser, his institution and others who had been members of that institution and been abused as members by senior leaders. The institution being the former Society of St Gerard Majella, the SSG, otherwise known as the Magellan Brothers. The leadership who had been charged and imprisoned for their offences were: Brother John Sweeney (Founder) and his associates Brother Joseph Pritchard and Brother Stephen Robinson. All of whom had been ordained Priests while still going by the title Brother. Stephen (SR) was the man in my case, the one I complained about through Peter Karp (PK).

Having refreshed you on these names, here continues the account of my engagement with the Towards Healing process.

Here I offer two accounts of meetings or facilitated negotiations which I had to endure as part of the 'process'.

Rosary Beads. (Bishop Anthony Fisher)
Somewhere in the middle of this process came the time to meet the bishop of Parramatta face to face. Although he wasn't bishop at the time of the abuse, he said he wished to apologise to me in person. I had to go all the way to his offices though, he wouldn't travel to me. I travelled alone that day and was met by Peter Karp and had a pre meeting briefing at the neighbouring Maccas where he had coffee and used the free Wi-Fi. Peter and I were greeted by office staff and shown into a small meeting room which was

furnished with a basic square table and four chairs, one on each side. A crucifix or some sad looking religious art hung over the table as if bearing witness to any matter disclosed within the four walls. We were offered a glass of water, no tea and biscuits such was the formality of this pastoral apology. There was a view through white lace curtains to the brick fenced plain garden beyond. Peter and I were kept waiting beyond the appointed time. A pool of perspiration formed under the palms of my hands and my arms stuck to the artificial veneer topped desk. I felt anxious, nervous and tense and glad my antiperspirant worked. I tried a mint which I had surreptitiously scavenged from the reception desk.

    Clanging sounds emanated from a distant corridor announcing the impending arrival of bishop Fisher. He wore his formal monk's robes of the Dominican Order, a cream-coloured full-length cassock and hood. The robe fastened by a black belt from which hung a pair of rosary beads constructed of heavy metal, bronze I'd say. Following the clanging and clashing of bead like bells his baby face appeared radiant as he graced us with his presence. Fisher was accompanied by an equally radiant and polished though severe face, that of the impeccably dressed lawyer, Mr Paul Davis. Despite his suit and formal attire, he looked like an elf trying his best to look tough. Davis carried a flat parcel wrapped in black and white clerical coloured glossy paper as if a Christmas gift but given at a wake. The gift was laid on the table in the corner between the bishop and the lawyer. The bishop looked lovingly at it and caressed it as if precious asking cryptically of the lawyer "is the special item enclosed?" Davis nodded knowingly - almost with a certain familiarity, to the bishop as they sat down. I was placed opposite the bishop, Davis to one side and Peter Karp to the other. Tension mounted as if a rider on a bull. Set was the scene for this pastoral apology.

    Davis outlined the agenda of what would happen and both lawyers left the room. Peter to Maccas and Davis to a place I'd rather not know or see for all I cared. Fisher remained opposite and asked me to say what I wanted. I said how I felt and showed him my old prayer book and a pair of well-worn wooden rosary beads which mum had given me at the age of 10 or so. They were smooth from use and soiled with sweat and the grime of my hands. I told him that these had meant so much to me but now only served as a reminder of the abuse at the hands of a cleric who had control over me. They reminded me of the harsh church, and I told him such symbols had negative meaning to me, far from devout pious holiness. He took them and felt them ever so briefly as if he needed a sanitising bath after touching that which I had touched.

Remaining in his seat, he then and spoke a recited 'apology' as if he'd mouthed the words many times before in similar situations with other victims of Clerical Sexual Abuse. He was too well practiced. He then slid the gift across, pushing it in my general direction as he slithered to the seat next to me at the side. There he gave me the envelope containing his formal of apology. No! Correction - the lawyer's form of apology. I don't believe for a moment the bishop nor any of his pastors composed the letter, though he did sign it personally and it was on his letterhead under the title:

"*Veritatem facientes in caritate*" or "Speaking the truth in love" he signed in green ink.

I read the letter in silence returning it to the envelope. I said "thankyou", for trying, not for a sincere apology. I never accepted it as an apology. I then forced myself to open the cheap little plastic pouch - knowing what it contained. Rosary beads! I stared in horror at them while he assured me "They are blessed by the Holy Father Himself." I cringed that Pope Benedict XVI - Józef Ratzinger himself had even been near these things given to me by Fisher. It was as if touching a cockroach in the mouth of a scorpion given me by a poisonous snake. Next was the glossy booklet, a complete history of the sandstone cathedral of Parramatta. I briefly, as if politely, skimmed the slippery pages, looking at images of colonial architecture, ultra-pious stained-glass windows and statues of St Patrick.

He thankfully refrained from any touch. I didn't detect any expression of care or concern for me or my situation. He seemed more concerned about his image and that of the church authorities. In my opinion he believed sincerely that this would be the end of the matter and I wouldn't be heard from again. A few weeks later I returned those gifts and refused the apology as you will read subsequently.

"Mr Facilitator"
The setting is a large conference room big enough to accommodate several hundred people, or the size of a basketball court. Not only was the hall booked but also a breakout room set up with tables of tea and coffee, water and juice accompanied with an array of biscuits and triangles of sandwiches. Our table for five was set up in the middle of the cavernous hall similar in size to that pictured here, but without windows to the world beyond. There was a balcony, but the outside temperature was in the high 30s that day. We were sweating enough!

Present were myself and Jennifer as my 'support person', my lawyer Peter Karp, the lawyer representing the Bishop, Mr Paul Davis, and our facilitator Mr Raymond Brazil. The Bishop, Anthony

Fisher chose to absent himself although in an office 200 metres away across the park.

    Mr Brazil took control of proceedings and got us to introduce ourselves although we had already met, though not in this context. He preferred to call us by our family names, but we all asked to be called by our given names. That's the only item we agreed with Mr Davis that day. Raymond called me "Paul – Paul Ward" and the other "Paul – Paul Davis". Raymond was happy to be called Raymond, though when addressed by the lawyers he was "Mr Facilitator". Such a formal beginning. There was more. We had to agree on who would take a break where and acknowledge it was to be awkward as we had to share spaces. Direct communication between the three of us and Mr Davis was forbidden and Mr Brazil being neutral was not to be addressed during breaks except for formal negotiation with one or both lawyers. During breaks he sat on a stool in the public foyer. Mr Davis was confined to the café area of the foyer.

    I sat opposite Raymond with Jennifer to my left, to her left was Mr Davis, then Raymond then to his left – my right was Peter Karp. The table was large enough to have three people a side. Plenty of space! Each of us had files, notes and stationery, though the facilitator only took brief notes in point form – therefore there was no transcript of the meeting.

I had been mentally prepared but as the hours dragged on, my brain became fuzzy and breaks were required. All the others were in full focus and Jennifer was a solid but mostly silent support throughout the day. I felt as if I was in the middle of a stage play and all this was happening around me, I had no real control. I was an actor within this horrid play. It was set up by lawyers and so formal. For heaven's sake! It was a pastoral situation gone horribly wrong. I was looking for a sincere apology for the sexual abuse of me by a former cleric of the diocese of Parramatta. I further sought an apology from Anthony Fisher for his treatment of me a month earlier. The church authority offered a 'financial gesture' of a set amount. Paul Davis had his fixed offer when we arrived, though he didn't outline it till after lunch. He was not going to budge or negotiate on the figure. A financial gesture had been offered some months earlier, but no amount had been mentioned. They asked me to suggest an amount for what I thought was compensation. I was looking for acknowledgement of past employment lost because of the abuse, missed opportunities, and so on. I needed to pay my lawyer a substantial amount, and the diocese had already agreed to pay my psychologist. The institution of the abuser had promised me a life of education, food and accommodation and clothing till death. But due to the abuse within that organisation I had, in my opinion and perspective, lost all those benefits. I felt badly done by to say the least. Rosary beads and an empty apology were not enough.

During the meeting I returned the rosary beads and the book asking the church lawyer to pass then back on to the bishop. He sounded offended saying the gift was given in 'good faith'. I said it had harmed me spiritually and socially and caused more angst toward the church.

I asked where the Bishop was and why he wasn't here. No satisfactory response except to say the lawyer was representing him. How could a lawyer represent a pastor in a pastoral situation? It was not pastoral we were told. Indeed, it wasn't.

On three occasions the Facilitator had to stand and order the lawyer for the church to leave the meeting and adjourn for fifteen minutes to calm down. On one such occasion I dared ask him "surely the church has to pay for my legal representative." He replied slamming his hand on the facilitation desk "the church does not have to do anything!" another time the churches' lawyer packed up his books and stood to leave. Jennifer grabbed his arm while Peter and Raymond pleaded him to remain in negotiation. He wanted to leave us, to turn his back on any negotiation. He was convinced to stay but after another fifteen-minute break.

The mood was as oppressive as the heat outside. We could escape the external heat but not that of the meeting. The church had booked the rooms till 4:30pm so a deadline loomed all day. As is typical of the church authority, all is left till the final minutes. The offer of financial gesture was made in the form of 'take it or leave it'. I was exhausted at the hands of that authority and had no other option but reluctantly and under duress take the offer. My team had a debriefing at the café before Jen and I headed back home - a two-hour trek.

Chapter 16
Personal Blooming
Turning 60

Marriage Equality became a major national movement causing many strained discussions on social media and around dinner tables eventually leading to great relief following a national vote on the subject. I was very much personally involved in the movement which had a deep and profound social and psychological effect on my life. The effect on me personally was like a rebirth, such was the struggle. A reinvention of my being, so to speak.

I had been divorced and living a single life in a retirement village, free to come and go and explore the world beyond marriage, beyond church, beyond traditional boundaries. I had to care for my own health and wellbeing and look after my finances too. The domestic life was kept simple, home cooking, doing my own washing and so on. Family were at arm's length too. That's the context of this profound change.

Social justice is a theme in my life from my time as a trainee Brother, Seminarian, mission volunteer, a youth worker and so on. Now I had time on my hands I attended several rallies in support of Asylum Seekers and Refugees, and several for 'Gay Rights', more correctly LGBTI or Queer rights, Queer recognition, the Sydney Gay and Lesbian MardiGras and the evolving Marriage Equality movement. I was very much 'getting out and getting involved' you might say. Attending the rallies, I listened carefully to the rally leaders and speakers, so motivational, so encouraging. I walked with groups behind banners. I sung and chanted rally cries. *"What do we want? Marriage Equality. When do we want it? Now!"*

Mixed in with this was the Royal Commission into Institutional Responses to Sexual Abuse of Children - The Child Abuse Royal Commission which I attended with earnest interest. There I met advocates for those abused by church and other institutions.

Some of those who attended included the retired NSW Police Officer - Peter Fox who I was honoured to chat with. Others were reporters from major media organisations including the Sydney Morning Herald and ABC News. Each day I had lunch in the courtyard with advocates for the abused including a lawyer from Broken Rites and others. We all shared our horror stories over coffee and hot lasagne or a meat pie. One particular attendee was Paul Davis, the lawyer for the Diocese of Parramatta! He and I came face to face at one tea break. He was near the window and I took full advantage of the close encounter on 'neutral' territory, albeit in a formal court, we were both struck to see each other after a few years. I button-holed him up close and suggested he knew more than he acknowledged. He expressed curiosity turning even more pink in the face now covered in a fresh glow of mild perspiration. I mentioned certain evidence regarding my time with the Brothers of St Gerard which he allegedly stored in cardboard cartons in his home garage, out of reach of Police and authorities who raided the Offices of the Bishop of Parramatta – then Bede Heather. Paul Davis denied any such cartons in his or any garage. I suggested they had since been destroyed and the contents shredded. The shredding of those documents is well documented elsewhere.

  Watching the Royal Commission at home, attending in person and reading the daily transcripts meant that I was very close to the proceedings and hearings. I pictured the 'actors' in the events including Cardinal George Pell, Bishop Bede Heather, Fr Brian Lucas and I could feel the atmosphere of their clandestine meetings of cover-up and denial. I never attended such meetings, there were secretive and restricted to clerics and their code of silence. However, as a student for the priesthood of the Archdiocese of Sydney, 20 years prior to this erupting, I sat on the Board of the Catholic Institute of Sydney as a Student Representative. I saw and heard how these clerics spoke and behaved. I was also on the 'inside' at the Seminary with direct access to clergy and leaders of the Church across NSW and Australia when they gathered for social events at Manly especially during the closing year celebrations in 1995. Living in presbyteries with priests also was a great insight into their lifestyle and attitudes. I have no doubt at all about any 'alleged' cover-up of their mates' sexual abuse of children, and adults. Although Adults over the age of 18 were excluded from the Commission of enquiry, the cover up would have similarly real and effective! All this had a profound effect on me as if I was abused all over again, including the working over through Towards Healing by Paul Davis and the Parramatta authorities including Bishop Anthony Fisher. I have mentioned him earlier.

As you can see, I was passionate about many and varied 'causes' or movements. It was at one Town Hall rally for Marriage Equality that I was particularly struck by a speaker, a young skinny gay man who didn't look particularly athletic or powerful but was inspirational and passionate. Most of the crowd of thousands were young people in their teens or twenties. Some may classify then as hipsters. I was a hipster at heart that day. The skinny guy asked us to look around at each other, he said there are hundreds of people like ourselves. He then talked of family and love. He was saying that we all come from loving families. He said our grannies love us as we are. People nodded and smiled. Me too, thinking of my elderly parents rather than grandparents. He said that in a loving family, people would most likely accept us as we are. This may have been over simplified but basically true. He said, if we wanted to in our own good time, we could Come Out to our grandparents simply saying we prefer to love people of the same sex as lovers or 'boyfriends / girlfriends' rather than people of opposite or different sex. That's the message I took away from the rally that Saturday afternoon.

    The rally moved into a march up Oxford Street from the Town Hall towards the gay flag at Taylor's Square. The left side of the road was closed to traffic so we could move freely along, though the downward side had traffic. I was part of the throng. Police guarded us and stopped us crossing the road into the traffic. Just then a bridal car approached, and I went toward it to grab a photo. A young policeman called out to me asking what I was up to. Saying I wanted to take a photo of the bridal car, he asked why. I said, because *they* can get married, but *we* can't. —

"Oh mate!", he exclaimed, understanding the social inequality. So simple, wasn't it?

Not so simple and clear to some.

Chapter 17
Retirement village life

Following the marriage separation, as you've seen, I moved into a Retirement Village. Before too long I had been elected Vice President of the residents' committee. We met monthly to discuss finances, plan events, lunches and parties and also to hear from management and advocate to the authorities on the concerns of the hundred or so others to whom we were responsible. We had two major annual dinners, Christmas and a mid-year event. These were catered by professionals associated with the local Bowling Club. The meat was thin, potatoes stale and dessert sweet. The entertainment was pretty good considering the amateur nature of the groups. Then there was the singalong. They still sung from a sheet of 1940s and 50s anthems. I tried to introduce ABBA or even the

Beatles but 'We'll meet again' was the all-time favourite.

Once a quarter a team of managers visited from Sydney to give the financial report and update on new developments for us and the wider community of the company. I often got the gig of handling the microphone so that all had a chance to be heard. Otherwise, I'd sit down at the back and try to keep the top brass to account. Once the CEO himself faced the locals. One woman stood and called him 'nothing but a weak little man'. Still, we scoffed down the stale triangle sandwiches, watered-down orange drink and insipid coffee before heading home to our villas for an afternoon nap.

Chapter 18
Grindr life

While at my retirement home watching Q&A on ABC24 one evening a Queensland National party politician by the name of Bob Katter stated that there are no homosexuals in his State. The young gay man to his left, Josh Thomas, responded saying there were indeed Gays in Queensland and there's an App for that called Grindr.

Within five minutes, I had downloaded it and signed up with a profile including brief personal description and a blury face pic. Line topics included:

interested in, not interested in, preferences for location to meet someone should it come to that and so on. I said my preference was men younger than myself, intelligent, socially aware, physically fit, respectful. I prefered to meet people socially in the first instance.

Within an hour I had several 'followers' and had begun chat conversations. For the first months it was about chat, I was trying to learn about life as a gay man, in particular in Sydney and that cities' northern region. The vast majority of contacts were in Sydney metro, with a few in my regional area of the Central Coast.

Thankfully the first contacts were a couple living locally who invited me for lunch in their garden. I went along as they stated they were committed and in a monogamous relationship. I listened carefully to their experience as a Gay couple living openly in the local community. They along with several others warned me that Grindr was by no means a safe place. There were many unscrupulous men using Grindr to trick others, to exploit them, for their own sexual and social desires. Here I also need to acknowledge the local social group of Gay men based around Gosford: 'Guys around Gosford'. I met them socially at the local RSL club and continued in their company for several years, meeting for dinner on Tuesday evenings at pubs and clubs in the local area. Sadly, some have since passed on, including the founder John. These men formed my social support network offering genuine friendship and care. Over dinner and drinks, we discussed food, politics, sexual abuse by church people, finances, and marriage equality. The social group was a very safe place for me during my exploring period, or Grindr years.

Another institution which was a solid support was the Central Coast Health office for Sexual Health. I attended psychological support sessions with the government funded psychologist on a regular basis over a period of several years. She helped me try to understand the nature of being Homosexual in the community and how to cope with my newfound arena of sexual interest and activity. The psychologist also listened carefully as I struggled with my former wife and my close family. There was a range of response to my 'coming out' from utter horror and shock, through tolerance, to acceptance and encouragement. The psychological help was wonderful, it was accompanied by sexual health checks coordinated by qualified and experienced nursing staff and sexual health doctors. Due to health risks associated with this period in my life, I had regular HIV and sexual health testing – all covered anonymously through the Australian and NSW Health care systems and funding. All the services were free of charge. Alongside this care I took advantage of ongoing mental health care which included my local GP and specialist relationship psychologists. I was still processing my sexual abuse from the age of nineteen along with the awakening of my sexual self as a homosexual man, the deterioration and breakup of my 'heterosexual' marriage and my moving into a Catholic based Retirement home. It was all happening!

Amid all this health care, I was on Grindr pretty much day and night. It became an obsession. My phone was never off, I suffered broken sleep and other mental and social problems.

I won't go into details but let's share some of my Grindr stories. Just for information so that you may see. You may find it disgusting, fascinating, unbelievable or repulsive. Upon reflection I found the overall experience an opportunity for learning, something which was detrimental to my social and mental health, an experience I would never wish to have again but also, I need to mention there were some few good men I met along the way.

So many times, it was like this: arrange to meet in a café for coffee or lunch. I'd be the one travelling because Sydney people can't go beyond their comfort zone. Two trains to a café and arrive in plenty of time not to keep him waiting. Find a table and sit there like a dill not ordering till he arrives. Who wants two coffees on a date? Is it a date? He arrives with apologies about not being able to find me, I feel as if he's blaming me for him being late. He constantly checks the time. I'm halfway through my coffee and he delays ordering lunch, it's only a sandwich! Then suddenly he realises he has forgotten he has a staff meeting which started 5 minutes ago and rushes off, leaving me to pay the bill. Then back on the train – a two-hour round trip for half a cup of coffee with a man I'll never see again! At least he turned up. Others would stroll by the café glancing in but passing by without even a greeting. So rude!

Then there were married men who were trapped in a marriage as a gay man but cheating on their beloved wives. Those poor women! Phone calls saying, 'sorry I'm late and I will get the milk and bread on the way back from this late board meeting'. Or requests from them for me to go "you'll have to go soon; I have to be home for the wife." Or meeting a man in his car outside the café because he is on a meal break from work or popped out to get stationery for the computer.

Another lot were too young for me, giving an older age on their profile. Skinny young fragile men who wanted to 'experiment' with an older man. They would try to be manly, to be all grown up but too much like a wilting flower when faced with a situation they had never handled. It must be tough for some younger gay men to admit they are gay and do something about it sexually. It was tough for me in admitting at the age of 60 as you have seen. I don't blame them. But OH!

Another lot were just out to make fun of me or those similar to myself. The ones who vanish in the dark, unseen. Then to appear in the carpark with mates laughing and jeering at me. I soon became wise to that type.

On the other hand, there were a few serious men who were in Australia for study or a good job, on a work visa. Some were of Arabic background, some middle eastern, some from strict religious communities, or strict cultures. One man told me he had to be secretive and very discreet because if his mother found out he is gay; she would be so shamed as to suicide. Another would be refused re-entry to his home country for fear of death or a life of torment and discrimination. These are the genuine cases of men I cared for and who sort true friendship rather than casual relationships. For a few we met two or three times, but it was so socially precarious that we could not meet again.

Some men frequented - in a sleezy way - 'haunts' such as certain institutions along Oxford Street in Sydney. Not my scene really.

Sydney gay MardiGras is another story! Love it. I only went once to the parade but have attended gay (and all the Acronyms) Fair Days.

The time I attended the parade I was prepared to go alone but thought it would be better to share with someone. The deal is that the route begins from Hyde Park where groups gather and are marshalled into position then they proceed up Liverpool Street, into Oxford St up to the top of the hill turning into Flinders Street and heading east a further kilometre towards Moore Park where the groups and floats disperse and party into the night. From the late afternoon the streets are lined with pedestrian and vehicle barriers as crowds form along the route grabbing vantage points. Shops, Pubs and nightspots are booked out months in advance. Some have VIP or paid seating out front or on balconies and roof tops. Media are set up along the route with vans and camera cranes. In the back lanes pop up food stalls are set up and one church has a BBQ in the yard with free food and drink for those who call by. Stalls sell coloured balloons, masks, and plastic crates for people to stand on. It's hectic for several hours. I had to get there early by train from the central coast and come prepared with a backpack of food and water and back up batteries for my phone. Dressing up is one thing, but sensible shoes are a must!

As it turned out, my friend in Taiwan knew a girl who is a student in Sydney who wanted to see the parade but who wanted to see it with a local. She and her female friend met me at Hungry Jacks on Oxford Street, and we found a table by the upper room window. Not so lucky as the restaurant was to close for the duration of the parade and we had to leave. Too late for a good spot in front of the now five deep crowd lining the streets. Drat. We walked up the hill, along the lanes and grabbed a free meal in the church yard before the cute bible preachers cornered us. We three eventually secured a front row spot about 200m from the end of the route. Good enough. We settled in with almost half an hour to spare. Once the *Dikes on Bikes* did their lap, we knew the excitement was soon to begin. It was quiet again for almost another half an hour before the first float or group reached us having covered the route from Hyde Park to us opposite the Captain Cook Hotel. Wow oh Wow! The girls are there for the sight of muscle men and hunky guys, me too. Glitter was everywhere, I had a rainbow of glitter on my face and more was thrown over the crowd across the next few hours. I managed to stand there for three and a half hours grabbing onto the fence which lined the centre of the road. At times I almost was pushed over or leant upon by other slightly more enthusiastic party goers. A few times I felt the arm of the man behind on my lower leg as he leant to grab a photo. I'd say he got pics of legs and feet mostly. Later in the night the dancers were tired but still marched on and put on a show for the cheering throng. At the close of the parade, we found a patch of grass behind us and sat for a picnic of fresh lychees and warm orange juice.

We then set out down toward Central Station with fellow weary but happy revellers. Taking the opportunity to speak openly with an actual gay Australian the Taiwanese girl asked heaps of questions about life in Australia and what it's like being gay. One question I'll never forget was typical of ignorant or innocent foreigners: In a gay couple of men, which one is the 'female' or feminine one?" I said that when a man and woman marry one is the husband and one the wife. Yes, they said. So, when two men marry, they are both husbands, and two women, both are wives. Oh, they saw the idea. Got it now.

The Fair day is held in a city park, open to all. Music and food are available but most of the focus is on information sharing from organisations such as banks, NSW Police, Professional counselling and care giving services and health agencies as well as LGBTI+ groups and organisations.

The pride march has evolved so much beyond the 1978 protest during which gay men and women were bashed by State Police. These days police and politicians join in on the festivities. Other groups represented are churches, major companies (possibly for marketing purposes), support groups and heaps of colourful dance teams. My favourite is the face painting as you can see! If you get a chance, I recommend visiting your local

Gay Pride activity. I do not recommend Grindr at all.

Chapter 19
Search for a new partner

As I write four or five years after the events to be told in this chapter, I can not help but ask myself: "What was I thinking?" !

I met two men via Grindr whom I followed back to their home countries, one The Philippines and the other Malaysia. The Filipino was younger than I but quite attractive and seemed mature for his age. He had a good job in Manila but lived a humble life in a gated community of people who couldn't afford good accommodation near the city. It was more of a slum area I'd say. The Malaysian was older than I and had retired and lived in a large triple storey house with a housekeeper, he also had a country residence, set in a tea growing area, with a full-time gardener.

Although the visits to The Philippines and Malaysia could be seen as a waste of money, much was learnt through the experiences.

These were nothing much more than holidays or excursions into SE Asia. There had been some feeling for the Filipino lad, he showed admiration for me too. The Malaysian gentleman on the other hand showed no feeling of admiration, no love and I felt nothing for him in a romantic sense. I did enjoy their hospitality and to some degree took advantage of the Malaysian with his welcome. I did share his birthday party with several others who seemed more interesting as people than he. His personality was not what I was looking for in a partner. Sure, he had money and a very comfortable life style, but how he related to others around him I found difficult. His maid fed the cats leftovers from the afternoon soirée and she was at his beck and call most of the day. Luncheon at the Penang Club with his closest friends was picturesque but for me quite awkward to endure, saved only by the banter of his guests and their inside jokes.

    The young Filipino on the other hand showed a much greater degree of hospitality, care and concern for me and my personal safety and comfort. His home was very basic, a single room with an attached wash room. We travelled to another island for a romantic getaway and I met his sister and her children. I felt very relaxed and welcome. Despite his care and hospitality and expressions of love, he was way too young for me and living in The Philippines was out of the question.

    The option of living in Asia was never realistic. I had to reconsider what I really needed as a person looking for a secure and lasting gay relationship in Australia.

    While all this was happening, the lust and love in SE Asia and the Grindr activity as well as genuine social engagement with the Guys Around Gosford, I continued my usual social activity at home with the old friends and on social media. Among the mix of all that, a man in Melbourne put me in touch with a friend of his who at the time was seeking a long-term relationship with a man such as myself. The new interest was Frankie, a Malaysian living in Melbourne who had sadly lost his long-term partner, Ken, a few years earlier. Frankie was ready to meet someone else and explore future possibilities.

Frankie and I corresponded by email and text message for several months, sharing information, our likes and dislikes in food, music, films, social interests, spirituality and so on. He had a good and steady job in Melbourne and was planning to settle and remain in Australia while at the time he was not yet a citizen, though he was on a Permanent Resident Visa. After some months we agreed it would be a good idea if I were to visit him at his place. Arrangements were made and I flew down with a bag of luggage, enough for a few weeks. I asked my neighbours to look out for my unit and collect my mail saying I'd return soon enough. It was the winter of 2017. A bitterly cold winter at that!

From Bateau Bay I took an early bus to the train station and a 90-minute trip down to Sydney Central where I changed to the Airport line. Alighting at Domestic, I walked through till I found the check in and departure lounge for my flight south, a journey of an hour and a half. It was late afternoon by the time I hit Melbourne. From Tullamarine airport I caught the bus to Spencer Street Station where I transferred once again to a suburban train and travelled to the end of the line at South Morang. I then had to pull my bag around a construction site at the shopping centre and find Kmart where I eventually stopped and put my feet up awaiting Frankie to see him for the first time. I was mentally exhausted and physically tired feeling a little grotty. My heart was bright and my mood was happy in anticipation.

      Soon enough a friendly sounding familiar voice greeted me from behind, albeit slightly tentative in tone but warm and welcoming and with a touch of tender care. "Hi, hello Paul, good to see you, how are you, are you hungry, are you ready to go." So many questions! I stood and turned slowly, happy but wearily. Putting out my hand, he shook it and we hugged briefly for the first time. Frankie pulled my bag out into the dark cold winter air and loaded it into his car. He was so excited as he drives the 20 minutes pointing out places of interest, I had trouble keeping up. We soon arrived at his home on the outskirts of Melbourne in the suburb of Mernda. I had a shower and he prepared dinner. I had arrived at last after leaving home around 6am that morning, it was now almost 7pm. It was an early night and we slept well after a chat in bed and a good night kiss. I felt comfortable, filled with joy and wonder.

Frankie worked five days a week so I was home alone most of the time, but without a car I was stranded but for local buses and walking. I spent time on my phone and tablet computer glad for the internet connection. At the time Mernda was several km from the rail terminus at South Morang which had a direct line to the city of Melbourne. South Morang was also home to the major shopping centre around the district. Mernda had 'Mernda Village Shops' including one supermarket, a discount chemist, a medical centre, Post Office, a café, cake shop, bakers, fish and chip shop, Thai restaurant and a Vietnamese takeaway. Oh, and a video rental machine. That's about it. Oh, and two dentists. No news agency, no fashion shops. Nothing much at all, just the basics. A rail station was promised as were a Police Station and an Ambulance Station too.

Frankie and I got on pretty well and we met a few other guys at house parties, restaurants in Richmond near the city and so on. Trips to the city were rare due to the transport arrangements. We spent the evenings after dinner watching movies or listening to music and chatting on the couch. We talked about many things, our personal histories and so on as I have mentioned.

After a week I returned back home to Bateau Bay full of excitement and wonder.

We kept in constant contact that Autumn and I was soon off back to Melbourne, this time by car. I drove via Mittagong and Gundagai then a night in Albury. This visit was to be longer than the first so I packed winter gear and a few sets of clothing and some photos and stuff. I felt that if it was to work out, I could leave stuff there to save repacking! I felt confident.

However, following a few cold winter months, I felt the need to return to Bateau Bay. I had the plan to go back there and give strong consideration to a future in Melbourne with Frankie. To facilitate a clear mind, I didn't leave anything behind and packed all my stuff in the car for the three-day return journey. My feeling was one of melancholy, sadness at leaving, not certain of returning or seeing him again. Perhaps I let negative feelings overwhelm me as I headed north east. I stopped by the road to cry a few times.

Once we were back in video contact I felt better and more confident.

It wasn't too long to wait to see Frankie again, this time it was his turn to visit me. He arrived by plane and I directed him by phone to the train from the airport, passing through Central Station where I boarded the train. We alighted at Museum where we once again embraced before heading off to a Malaysian restaurant for a late lunch. I was so glad to see him and hear his voice and share a meal once again. Frankie stayed with me a few days in my little villa while we toured the Central Coast.

The highlight in my opinion was seeing him play among the rock pools at the beach. He gazed in sheer joy and amazement at the life which inhabited them. Slimy green fresh moss, little creatures which live in shells and the sweet smell of salt water. Upon his return to Melbourne, I was again sad but filled with hope in our future together. We decided that I should return to Mernda but this time not till I had packed up and cleared out from dear Bateau Bay. A very positive outcome from the visit!

Meanwhile, in early December 2017, Frankie's parents visited him from Malaysia staying in his visitors' room. He proudly showed them around the city and his local area. It was the first time they had travelled overseas. While they visited, I was busy selling off furniture and giving away clothing and stuff such as my collection of original mid-70s coffee mugs.

A vital and cathartic part of my culling and chucking out was the destruction of and throwing away of my files relating to the sexual abuse, the church links and all those dark memories. I was glad and felt a physical relief to get rid of them. Into the communal recycling bin, they went! Somewhat symbolic being in a catholic institution where I lived in retirement compared to that catholic institution where I lived as a teenager some 40 years earlier.

The move to Melbourne also meant a clear break from close family and dear friends in Sydney and on the Central Coast. I would not be returning to live in NSW, at least for many years, if ever. I bad my farewells to everyone. There were moments of joyful reflection and heaps of well wishes too. Mum was by then in the early stages of dementia and didn't quite understand the significance of my move to Melbourne. Dad was 'getting on' but still active in his bowling club and in contact with a support network. I just had to leave them and go. I knew they were in good hands, including with Cathy as their legal guardian and others around. I could visit at times as well as call and write emails and leave messages on Facebook and Instagram. It was time to move on, towards a fresh beginning. I was somewhat used to fresh beginnings but this would be major, moving in with a new Life Partner in an 'openly gay' relationship. I was 'out' and moving away from my past.

Chapter 20
Move to Mernda

I sent most of my gear on the back of a van which arrived ahead of me and Frankie stored it in the garage till I arrived a few days later. His parents had left just before the stuff arrived and I was not far behind. My drive south took three days, they were days and nights full of anticipation and glad hope for a beautiful future life in Melbourne. The road took me around Sydney, south through NSW bypassing Canberra and down to Albury where I spent my last night before crossing into Victoria and pushing down to Wangaratta for a coffee break and snack, then on to the outskirts of Melbourne where I turned onto the last stretch which happened to be the only dirt road in the whole trip. Both sides of the road are pasture fields with grazing cattle. The road then enters the settled urban zone bound by a wire backyard fence. This is Mernda on the Rural Urban fringe.

Frankie was there out front of the house to greet me with is welcoming smile and helping hand. We unpacked my car and after a fresh hot shower we had a warm coffee before he prepared a special 'welcome home' dinner. There was much to talk about and heaps of unpacking over the next days as well as preparing for Christmas 2017. This was my first Christmas in Melbourne and Frankie had already put up the Christmas tree in the living room.

He was soon back to work between the Christmas - New Year days and then we were into a routine at home. I found myself doing the household tasks of washing and shopping while he worked some distance away in his I.T. support job at an aged care facility.

We were now growing together as Partners rather than Boyfriends. I came to call Frankie by his Chinese name – Cheng Wee, though at work and among others he was always Frankie. With the movement of time, we established a garden. We planted a vegie patch, a passionfruit vine and several native bushes around the place. One of our favourite occasional outings was to the markets at La Trobe University car park where we bought our plants and fresh fruit and vegetables and a few odds and ends. One particular Sunday Cheng Wee paused at the fish stall and looked lovingly and deeply with a sweet smile suggesting we get a gold fish. We did have artificial fish in a round fish bowl but they weren't real and the batteries went flat after a while. So, listening to the advice of the sales man we brought home several small fish of various colours which lived in the little tank till we got a larger one. Eventually we dug a pond in the back corner of the garden. It was not easy going and a bit of a male bonding exercise. The ground is clay mud which stuck to our gum boots and gloves. Five small fish at an initial cost of $10 turned into a major project. We had to feed them, clean the pond, filter the water, check the pH levels, protect them from prey in the form of a grey heron and decorate the pond area with stones, pavers and appropriate plants. The house became a home. Cheng Wee had said he felt alone and lonely and not inclined to do gardening or decorating. We now formed a family, just the two of us, but family none the less. Some tired old furniture went out and new furniture blended in. We set up an office in the empty room, moved the old bed to a spare room for visitors and got a new one for ourselves. Some art works brightened the walls while the growing garden brightened the exterior.

Chapter 21
Getting active in Victoria

Meeting other gay men through friends was my initial introduction to fellow Victorians. There's no social organisation as such, but a loose network of friends, people who know people. The first event in December 2017, was a quiet Christmas party at a friends' home in suburban Melbourne where half a dozen of us gathered for a hot roast lunch around a traditionally set dining table, followed by singing along to music videos and some impromptu dancing. From this group I was introduced to others at Easter weekend parties, Melbourne Cup lunches and the famous 'Festive' parties where I met several women and men associated with cinema and stage. None were really 'close' friends, rather familiar acquaintances who shared pleasant conversation, opinions and personal stories of times past. One or two remained constant friends across the years 2017 to 2021. Most remained in the background of that loose circle of acquaintances while some were never to be seen again.

It was in the wider community of older locals that I felt more at home. I saw advertised a talk for seniors on retirement planning or something similar so I went along to the local Community Centre. The talk was interesting enough and afternoon tea was pretty good too. Someone asked if I was a member of the Doreen and Mernda Coffee Club for Seniors or some other group. I said I had just recently arrived here and asked about it. I was instantly surrounded by women from the group who invited me to their morning coffee the following Tuesday. Feeling the need to socialise with others around the locality, especially those around my age bracket, I took up the offer. Two weeks later they had lunch at the pub so I went along having had a positive feeling about them. Nothing like a wine and hot roast to get people of my generation chatting. **They were all 'Baby Boomers' and I felt right at home!**

This was the early formation of the Doreen Baby Boomers. It was an online group which developed and grew by word of mouth and personal invitation amongst similar aged people - i.e., Late 50s to early 70s - give or take a decade! Most had gone to school in the 1960s and 1970s, and disco dancing in the 70s and 80s, endured the 1990s and celebrated the Millennium. Most had been or still were married, with grandchildren, some had moved on or had lost their partner. There was heaps in common and shared history among us. I became a regular member attending the coffee and cake mornings and the lunches at the Pub. Several times I joined some of the others in walking. On a couple of occasions such as Christmas time shared lunch, Cheng Wee came along with me. We were accepted as who we were, a gay male couple. Not many tall younger gay Asian men around here either, it has to be said.

The Baby Boomers grew in number from a large table of us to several tables to the point we booked out the complete upper floor of the local 'Slices' restaurant for our monthly morning cuppa gatherings which sometimes included invited guest speakers.

It was during this period that I did visit Mum and Dad and the family in Sydney and sadly Mum passed away after a few weeks in hospital. Cheng Wee came with me to her funeral and wake.

Following the passing of mum, Dad toured visiting relatives in NSW and Queensland usually accompanied by Cathy and Graz or some of the others. Soon he expressed his interest to visit us in Mernda and specifically asked to meet the Baby Boomers! As it turned out the BB had arranged the end of year Christmas dinner at Slices around the time of his visit in December 2019. I booked us in. What an evening! Cheng Wee and I danced with the others as Dad enjoyed the music and seeing the action on the dance floor. No doubt he was missing mum, this being the first Christmas without her in 65 years. We had photos taken and enjoyed the meal and drinks. That was the last big party for dad. He returned to Sydney a few days later. Cheng Wee and I went up for the family Christmas lunch at the old house. There was happiness in the room where the family had traditionally gathered for many celebrations over the years. A tinge of sadness was about the room to as Mum was with us and we knew Dad was soon to leave as well. He passed away in an aged care home early the following February at the age of 92.

Some weeks after the funeral I shared a cuppa with the Boomers as they listened to my account of the death and funeral of my father.

Shortly after that at in March of 2020, without much notice, all that socialising came to an abrupt holt due to Covid19 restrictions on public gatherings. Social Distancing morphed into Physical Distancing so even the walks were off due to the 1.5 metre rule, mask wearing and no mixing of people from different households. The Facebook group continued during 'lockdown periods' and when the restrictions lifted, we did get back to cuppa times and walking.

Chapter 22
Covid 19

Late in 2019 a new mystery virus developed in the Wuhan Province of China, most likely in a so called 'wet market' where live animals are sold to buyers as fresh meat. An animal virus somehow infected a human who unwittingly passed it on to others nearby. Thus, this new or 'novel corona' virus began its invidious spread across the entire planet within a few deadly weeks. The virus became to be known as Coronavirus, or Covid19.

Soon Australia, like others, began to impose bans on immigration or travel from China. However, as it spread to Europe and other continents the travel bans eventually became universal. Australia closed its international borders to all tourists and business travellers from all countries. The major exception being for returning Australians who had to enter quarantine in Quarantine Hotels for two weeks at the expense of the State Government (the taxpayer). Months later the governments realised the huge expense and then required late comers to pay their own quarantine costs. Meanwhile a cruise ship, the Ruby Princess carrying Australian tourists allowed many passengers to disembark in Sydney. The federal government Boarder Security check for Customs and the usual quarantine such as fruit and uncooked food. They failed to do proper health checks for possible Covid19 cases, sheeting the blame to the NSW State dept of Health. The bottom line was that over 1700 passengers disembarked at Circular Quay and took buses, trains, taxies and other means of transport to their homes and went about their business shopping and socialising unrestrained. Covid spread through the unsuspecting local community infecting the most vulnerable older and frail population indiscriminately.

We were told to distance ourselves in public places and try our best to keep 1.5 metres apart. This practice came to be known as Social Distancing or Physical Distancing as mentioned earlier. The aim of physical distancing was to 'flatten the curve' of 'cases' as described in graph chart form. Some venues such as Pubs were closed, some restaurants and cafés could only have a certain number of customers and stores had limits of one customer per 4 Sq. metres. While the aim was looking to a form of recovery known as a 'return to normal' it was soon clear that there would be no 'return' but a 'new normal' or Covid Normal. Life as we knew it had changed for ever.

Supermarkets were stripped of goods - firstly bathroom stationery, then pasta and rice, then supplies of fresh meat and vegetables dwindled to levels such as to be listed as: 'scarce or unavailable'. Fights among customers erupted in the paper goods aisles over toilet paper.

Product limits were enforced at the checkouts. A few shoppers began wearing plastic gloves to touch everything to no effect at all but drive up the sale of gloves. Eventually supply chains caught up to the panic buying demand and we had a glut of toilet paper for a few weeks.

In order to try to combat the virus many different restrictions were set in place and hierarchies of restrictions were formed. Phase 1 was the Physical Distancing and personal hygiene step. Keep 1.5m and sneeze into a handkerchief or the elbow. House parties and other large gatherings were discouraged or limited to close family and friends. Weddings and Funerals were also limited in number and had to keep to the distancing rules. No hugging or holding hands. Churches and other places of worship were also regulated for crowd size and eventually closed.

It's amazing how thousands of devout practising Catholics who believe in the holy Obligation to attend and celebrate Eucharist every weekend all of a sudden stopped going to church. It used to be an obligation under the fear of social and spiritual death, excommunication! However, if forbidden by the secular government, ok, time to sleep in on Sundays. If only the secular obligation to report abuse within the church were honoured by church authorities and bishops, when told by Government authorities - but not to be. Protect the 'church' at any cost including: suicide or damaging mental health of those abused.

Meanwhile the mental and social health of we Australians suffered due to even more strict Stage 2 then Stage 3 restrictions.

Daily, we Victorians are reminded by all the other States and Territories that they do not want us to enter. We are forbidden to cross the border into any adjoining jurisdiction. 'Corona Hot Spot' is now the new 'Leper Colony' of Biblical times. We have a legal and health wall around us. Some have dared try to journey into other territories only to be stopped or uncovered and be issued with fines up to $1600.00 and similar. When South Australia to the west blocked us, our **Premier Dan Andrews said "who wants to go to SA anyway? Be a tourist in Victoria."** That was before Melbourne became a Victorian Hot Spot. Then Dan banned his own citizens from travelling beyond the metro area into regional Victoria. This week (early August 2020), Dan declared a State of Disaster (up from State of Emergency), so now we have the latest a Level 4 lockdown in Metro Melbourne, covering about 5 million people. The state of Disaster will be enforced for a set period of six weeks till the end of September. Police have extraordinary powers to stop and question people and to issue on-the-spot fines for breach of Covid regulations as declared by the Government. Stage 4 means a night curfew between 20:00 and 05:00 the next day. Residents need a permit to be out on the streets during curfew hours and can only be out if going to or from work or a hospital. We are only allowed exercise for up to an hour a day and are not permitted to go shopping in groups, one at a time at the supermarket or grocery or butchers. All other retail such as clothing and furniture shops will be closed for six weeks from tomorrow 6th August 2020. Cafes and restaurants are open for take away only and the food or drinks cannot be consumed in public due to the mandatory mask rule. A good by-product of all this is that by default or happy fault - smoking in public is also ruled out and gambling is out too as pubs and clubs are closed for the duration.

For those with Covid 19 - i.e., Covid Positive - they have to remain in their residence for two weeks, no going out unless to Hospital and as Dan says, if you are that ill with Covid, you will be in an ambulance, not driving or in a car or taxi. They are permitted to get fresh air by opening a window or standing at an exterior door. Military personnel are supporting teams of health inspectors who door knock every 'positive case' residence. They offer assistance with essential shopping or pharmacy needs and offer to connect patients with health care and other care givers. However, if they are not home as required Police are sent to knock on the door and if still not home, they are issued a fine for being in contravention of the Stay-at-Home order.

Each premier or state leader and the PM and their health advisors front the media almost daily. Premier Dan has had a one-hour media conference every day for the past four months or so. Dan is so focussed and promises to answer every media question. Yesterday he became so frustrated that he said, "I need to take a deep breath." Today after persistent questioning from one reporter on her one topic he paused and said "I need to move on and give the others a chance to ask questions on other topics, however if you want to continue, I am happy to stand here for two hours, not that I am suggesting you continue." He eventually got to address more points on public health. She backed off till tomorrow.

All the news is: vision of police and military patrolling the empty streets, people in hospital, citizens speaking of recent deaths in the family, aged care homes with ambulances queued up taking residents to hospital and funeral cars taking them out in pine boxes. All that and more is so depressing to me and my partner and others in the community. The Covid effect on mental health is a real phenomenon. Tele-health consultations are not adequate. People are suffering in silence. The human effects of this Covid Crisis will go on for years yet.

The economic crisis is another story. Businesses fail due to closure. Workers are jobless and on social security payments. The government is literally spending billions on social welfare and support for business. Treasurers and company financers say we will be paying for this for decades to come. Let's hope we don't face other disasters in coming years.

Covid UPDATE: September 2021.

Since writing my first edition a year ago Australia remains in the grip of Covid, though we seem to be nearing the end of this human tragedy.

Victoria is now in our sixth period of Lockdown. There was only two weeks of relief between Lockdown 5 and Lockdown 6. During Lockdown 4, Covid case numbers reached a peak of 750 new cases a day with several deaths reported regularly. Due to the efforts of the authorities and cooperation of the community, those numbers went down to 50, then 20 then eventually sat on 5 a day for a while. The restrictions were called off indefinitely though we still had to carry a mask, most retail and pubs were open again. Life seemed to be 'Covid normal'. Meanwhile others Sates suffered and a NSW taxi driver contracted Covid from an international flight crew member of a cargo flight. That driver passed it on to family in Bondi and to others in western Sydney. From there three truck drivers brough it unknowingly across the border into Victoria! Now it was the 'Delta variant' which spread like wild fire across the State. Delta Covid had hit the two biggest capitals in Australia. Sadly, NSW is recording around 1500 cases daily and Victoria is a few weeks behind with 500 a day as I write in late September 2021. The encouraging news is the development and distribution of several Vaccines. Last year in the better times, the federal government declared it was not a race to get vaccinated, so supplies were not ordered in time. Delta took control! However, we do now have growing percentages of people vaccinated. The program is that once 70% of the eligible population over 16 are vaccinated, then at 80%, there are promised 'rewards' or easing of restrictions. We can now travel up to 10km compared to 5km as it has been in recent months. Masks remain mandatory. Some industries such as Health, Hospitality and Construction are becoming Vaccine mandated. Cheng Wee and I are double vaccinated. Soon we all will have to carry an electronic 'Covid Passport' to prove we are fully vaccinated before entering stores and other venues. Also, as most of the population over 50 have had a single dose and many have had their second dose, Covid is now a disease of the young and unvaccinated across Australia.

By Christmas 2021 we will have developed a two-class society: Those who are fully vaccinated and those who are not.

I have to sign off for now. My hope is that this will be a social record for you dear reader and your descendants.

Chapter 23
Family moments

Family events have overtaken the writing process. Events which need to be addressed. A life memoir cannot be complete without a chapter on family as it has evolved recently.

As you have read earlier my dear parents passed away in recent years.

Whatever is written, whatever I say can ever be a full and complete description of my parents and family. Words are not enough.

I was born in October 1954, first born child after the tragic loss of my brother John before he had a chance to see the light of day and draw breath. Mum and dad suffered this dreadful memory for almost 70 years. I cannot begin to imagine the feeling. He was taken from mum without a chance to hold him and buried in an unmarked grave with other little children in a corner of Botany Cemetery. Mum and Dad told me of him when I was a young boy.

That's why mum Baptised me as soon as I got home. Don't tell the old Irish Missionary Priest. He got the 'official' duties but Mum saved my eternal soul from life in Limbo. That was her belief and that of the Church till recently. She was so glad to hear Limbo is a theological construct. God is Love and would never punish a person for no fault of their own. So glad the Church has moved on from such silly thought and teachings.

Mum and Dad celebrated new life in the birth of each of us and our milestones such as First Communion, Confirmation, first jobs, their grandchildren, engagements and weddings. They were with us in our struggles and joyful times. Mum and Dad always supported my although they were often confused or didn't understand. My earlier strides into church life were welcome and supported as good catholic parents would. However, when I announced, I was engaged to Jennifer after years living in a Seminary - the sheer joy on their faces! To be seen! It was such a relief I guess, to them; they physically clapped and slammed the kitchen table in joy and offered me a second cup of tea! Ok, so not so animated but they were happy.

It was with sadness but some understanding from them when Jennifer and I visited and revealed to them that we had come to the decision to separate. As was my practice I put it in writing. Mum read the letter carefully in silence. Patting the page, she looked up at us saying "this is sad". A few months later they visited me in my new home unit at Bateau Bay. They saw that it was a good place and I'd say they felt satisfied I was in a good place socially, psychologically and physically. It being a Catholic institution helped them too. Also, I was living close by to Jennifer and they were not far away. They never visited again. They visited us - Jennifer and I - at Umina several times, once shortly after we settled in, for Christmas 1997 and occasionally around Mothers' Day. Going back in time, they visited me once at Manly, once at Earlwood and once at my flat in Hillsdale in 1976. Oh, but that time mum stood at the door and handed over my birthday present - she didn't enter as there were people drinking and smoking. Same as when another relative got engaged, they didn't go in due to others drinking and smoking. Mum's dad worked at a brewery for years, he joked that he sampled the beer! Mum did sample a sparkling wine at Umina, she said she wanted to see what all the fuss was about. One sip! No, she didn't like it. Others at the table were drinking so I guess she endured it for the afternoon. As she aged into her late 80s, mum became more tolerant of drink at parties and celebrations. At her 90th I don't think she noticed at all. By that time, she didn't notice it was Sunday and she was not at church. Such was her sad state of dementia.

In late November 2020, Cheng Wee put up our Christmas tree once again. Last year dad was here. It's now a point of memory for us. The week dad came and stayed with us. Christmas 2021 will be another anniversary. Two years since our final family Christmas at the old home. Sad that mum was not with us in person. Sad that we knew it would be the last with dad around the old family table in the back room. Joyful for the fond memories of the family in the old home.

Time moves on. My life continues into an unknown but exciting and confident future with my dear Frankie - Cheng Wee.

Long may we live to work through another chapter or two together. Perhaps it will be written in another decade.

www.ingramcontent.com/pod-product-compliance
Lightning Source LLC
Chambersburg PA
CBHW030253010526
44107CB00053B/1694